101 Questions and Answers on
the Eucharist

101 QUESTIONS AND ANSWERS ON THE EUCHARIST

Giles Dimock, OP

Paulist Press
New York/Mahwah, N.J.

Unless otherwise noted, the scripture quotations outlined herein are from the New Revised Standard Version Bible: Catholic Edition, copyright 1989, 1993, Division of Christian Education of the National Council of the Churches of Christ in the United States of America. Used by permission. All rights reserved.

Cover design by Cynthia Dunne

Library of Congress Cataloging-in-Publication Data

Dimock, Giles.
    101 questions and answers on the Eucharist / Giles Dimock.
        p.   cm.
    Includes bibliographical references.
    ISBN 0-8091-4365-8 (alk. paper)
    1. Lord's Supper–Catholic Church. 2. Mass. 3. Catholic Church—
Doctrines. I. Title.
BX2215.3D56 2006
234'.163 — dc22

                                                                    2006004237

Published by Paulist Press
997 Macarthur Boulevard
Mahwah, New Jersey, 07430

www.paulistpress.com

Printed and bound in the
United States of America

CONTENTS

THE 101 QUESTIONS AND ANSWERS

ABBREVIATIONS OF THE SOURCES

A.A.   *Apostolicam Actuositatem.* Decree on the Apostolate of Lay People. Vatican II, 1965.

B.L.S.   *Built of Living Stones: Art, Architecture and Worship.* NCCB, 2000.

CCC   *Catechism of the Catholic Church.* USCC, 1994.

C.I.C.   *Codex Juris Canonici.* The Code of Canon Law, 1983.

D.C.   *Dominicae Cenae.* Apostolic Letter on the Eucharist. John Paul II, 1980.

D.D.   *Dies Domini.* Apostolic Letter on Sunday. John Paul II, 1998.

D.S.   Denzinger Schömmetzer, *Enchridion Symbolorum Definitorum Declarationem.* Herder, 1965.

E.E.   *Ecclesia de Eucharistia.* Encyclical on the Eucharist. John Paul II, 2003.

GIRM   General Instruction of the Roman Missal. 2000.

HCEWOM   Holy Communion and Eucharistic Worship outside Mass: The Rites. 1976.

I.C.   *Immensae Caritatis.* Document of the Congregation of the Sacraments on the Minister of the Eucharist. 1973.

I.I.   *Inter Insignores.* Document on the Ordination of Women. CDF, 1976.

L.G.   *Lumen Gentium.* Dogmatic Constitution on the Church. Vatican II, 1964.

M.D.   *Mulieris Dignitatem.* Apostolic Letter on Women. John Paul II, 1988.

Mem. Dom.   *Memoriale Domini.* Paul VI, 1976.

M. F.   *Mysterium Fidei.* On the Holy Eucharist. Paul VI, 1965.

N.A.   *Nostra Aetate.* Declaration on Non-Christian Religions. Vatican II, 1965.

R.S.   *Redemptionis Sacramentum.* 2004.

S.C.   *Sacrosanctum Concilium.* Constitution on the Sacred Liturgy. Vatican II, 1963.

S.T.   *Summa Theologiae* of St. Thomas Aquinas, OP.

U.R.   *Unitatis Redintegratio.* Decree on Ecumenism. Vatican II, 1964.

INTRODUCTION

I have been a priest for more than thirty-five years, and most of that time I have been a professor of liturgy and sacraments. I've been fortunate in teaching in the States and in Rome, both on the graduate and undergraduate levels. I've taught in New England, Ohio, and in the nation's capital, as well as lecturing in parishes, for prayer groups, and appearing on television, and everywhere people have questions. Bright undergrads have questions; puzzled grad students have questions; questioning professionals and praying housewives have questions; people call up with questions; and for my whole academic life I've enjoyed fielding questions — sometimes well, sometimes ineptly. It's natural for us, gifted with minds seeking truth that God gave us, to ask questions. It is not a sign of skeptical doubt, but I think an exercise of "faith seeking understanding" — St. Anselm's definition of theology. I believe, but faith goes beyond human reason and sometimes *seems* to contradict it, and therefore I ask questions so that I might believe more firmly. And so the Catechism of the Council of Trent asked questions; Martin Luther asked questions in his catechism; the *Baltimore Catechism* asked questions, and in these catechisms, answers were given. The *Catechism of the Catholic Church* (which does not use the traditional question-and-answer format), the *Constitution on the Sacred Liturgy* of Vatican II and later official Vatican documents, the doctrinal pronouncements of the Church on the Eucharist, the teaching of John Paul II in his eucharistic encyclical *Ecclesia de Eucharistia,* and the insights of my elder brother, St. Thomas Aquinas, will all come to my aid as I attempt to answer the eucharistic questions I have most often encountered in my teaching and preaching. May this attempt, aided by the Holy Spirit, help in affirming and understanding (to the degree that one can) the great mystery of Christ's presence among us in this sacrament.

ONE

JEWISH BACKGROUND: BEGINNINGS

1. When was the Eucharist instituted?

"At the Last Supper, on the night he was betrayed Our Savior instituted the Eucharistic sacrifice of his Body and Blood. This he did in order to perpetuate the sacrifice of the Cross throughout the ages until he should come again, and so to entrust to his beloved Spouse the Church, a memorial of his death and resurrection: a sacrament of love, a sign of unity, a bond of charity, a Paschal banquet 'in which Christ is consumed, the mind is filled with grace, and a pledge of future glory is given to us'" (S.C. 47).

This quotation from the Constitution on the Sacred Liturgy answers our question and gives not only the reason why he did so, but also an idea of the breadth and depth of the mystery we shall be examining together.

Jesus, the Son of God, born into the Jewish milieu as a human, fulfilled all of the requirements of the Torah or the Jewish law. He observed the Passover celebration, a memorial of the escape of the Hebrews from Egypt, and he gave this sacred meal a new meaning that is explicated in the quote above, namely that the Eucharist would make the Sacrifice of the Cross present as he fed his Church in the future with his Body and Blood as food and drink.

2. Is the Eucharist only a meal?

A meal is defined as eating together and in order. The Eucharist is a special meal that has been described as a banquet by St. Thomas Aquinas in an antiphon in the Liturgy of the Hours for the feast of Corpus Christi: "O Sacrum Convivium"—O Sacred Banquet—but the Eucharist is much more than a meal. Meals satisfy the human need of being together, not just the biological need of nourishment for the body. In some sense all meals are sacrificial, because in eating I consume something that has given up its animal or vegetable life for me, be it a chicken or a head of lettuce. Sacred and sacrificial meals were the way that ancient peoples often showed their dependence on the gods, offering animals, pouring out wine, offering bread and wine (the Greeks), eating bread (the Aztecs), and the Hebrews used some of these same rituals to commune with God. Exodus 24 describes how Moses and the elders ratified the Covenant on Mount Sinai by slaughtering young bulls in sacrifice, splashing their blood (the sign of life) on twelve pillars representing the twelve tribes of Israel, and then how the seventy elders and Moses ate a sacrificial meal in the presence of God (Exod 24:11). We must see the Last Supper against this background.

John Paul II made clear in his encyclical *Ecclesia de Eucharistia* that to see the Eucharist "stripped of its sacrificial meaning...celebrated as if it were simply a fraternal banquet" is a "reductive understanding" and therefore not the Catholic understanding of the Eucharist (no. 10).

3. Is there a connection between the Jewish Passover and the Eucharist?

God commanded the Israelites in the Book of Exodus to keep the Passover feast (or Pasch) in memory of their deliverance from Pharaoh (Exod 12). In general, the structure of this sacred sacrificial meal involved the washing of hands, bitter herbs to remind the Israelites of their slavery in Egypt, the explanation of the symbolism of the foods to be eaten, the blessing and distribution of wine and unleavened bread, the eating of the paschal lamb with joy and festivity, and a particularly solemn blessing said over the Cup of Blessing by the father of the family or the one presiding at this banquet. This great prayer of praise and blessing or *berakah* prayer blessed God and thanked him for all of the blessings the Israelites enjoyed, especially their freedom from slavery in Egypt and their *Exodus* or coming out of Egypt into the Promised Land.

The synoptic Gospels, Matthew, Mark, and Luke, set the Last Supper of Jesus in this paschal or Passover setting. John has a slightly different perspective. Perhaps John, the Theologian as he is called in the East, is more concerned with showing Jesus as the paschal Lamb of God (John 1:29), whose death could be compared to those lambs being prepared for slaughter for the Passover that had not yet happened (John 18:28, 19:31). Some try to make all accounts agree by contrasting different ways of computing when Passover actually began at that time. In any event the paschal (Passover) symbolism was in the air, and the Synoptics take it up as does St. Paul as he proclaims, "For our paschal lamb, Christ, has been sacrificed," (1 Cor 5:7) and this Passover symbolism is the backdrop of the Last Supper.

Jesus, as a good Jew, observes the ritual, but in blessing the unleavened bread, he gives it new meaning: it becomes his Body. The Cup of Blessing (cf. 1 Cor 10:16) becomes his Blood, "which will be shed for you" (Matt 26:28; Mark 14:24; Luke 22:20), linking the Last Supper with the Crucifixion to come the next day. This establishes the "new and everlasting covenant" (the Words of Institution at Mass; cf. Matt 26:28; Mark 14:24; Luke 22:20) replacing the old, with the twelve apostles rather than the twelve tribes, and this is to be done as a memorial, or "in remembrance of me" (Luke 22:19; 1 Cor 11:25), in the Jewish context and the Jewish understanding of memorial we shall have occasion to explore later.

Two

Names of the Eucharist

4. Why is this sacrament called the Eucharist?

We just described how the Israelites of old, like the Jews of today, prayed prayers of *berakah,* praise and thanksgiving for God's deliverance of them from the slavery of Egypt and leading them into the Promised Land, and that the Lord Jesus preserved this ritual at the Last Supper while giving it a radically new meaning. The apostles and the first followers of the Lord in their sacramental meals gave thanks as well, but for deliverance from sin and its slavery into the kingdom of God through the death and resurrection of Christ made present in this holy meal in the Lord's Body and Blood. *Eucharistia* means "thanksgiving," and as we celebrate this sacramental and sacrificial meal, we give "thanks" *through* Jesus' great act of praise and thanksgiving, his death on the cross and the Father's acceptance of that in the resurrection made present in this meal. So we call this great sacrament the Eucharist, or thanksgiving.

The Eucharist is named for many aspects of the Mystery at its core and the *Catechism of the Catholic Church* explains many other names (cf. CCC nos. 1328–32). We shall explore only a few.

5. Why is the Eucharist called the Mass?

As the apostles evangelized and as St. Paul converted Gentiles (non-Jews), the core of the Eucharist (the blessing: thanksgiving over the bread and wine) remained, but in different cultures variations in ritual and language naturally began to take shape. In Rome, the Eucharistic Liturgy was celebrated in Greek until the fourth century. When it was celebrated in Latin, gradually various Roman customs began to be adapted to the liturgy. At the end of a Roman ceremony all were dismissed with the stylized phrase: *Ite missa est:* "Go, it is finished." This phrase became popular and the phrase for "it is finished," *missa est,* began to

9

have a life of its own, with *missa* becoming popular not just as a way to describe the dismissal but the whole eucharistic rite. *Missa* in Latin becomes *messa* in Italian, *misa* in Spanish, *messe* in French, and *mass* in English. The *Catechism* sees the dismissal of Mass as sending us forth on "mission" *(missio)* from our participation in the mystery of salvation going forth to do God's will (CCC no. 1332) and to preach the good news (Mark 16:15).

6. Why is the Eucharist called the Blessed Sacrament?

The seven sacraments are believed to have been given us by the Lord Jesus Christ. They are outward signs using water, oil, bread, wine, etcetera, and they are signs of the inner reality of God's life in the same way that the humanity of Christ is a sign of his divinity. While Christ was on earth he brought about many miracles, effected many healings that a human alone could not effect. His divinity worked through his humanity and accomplished signs and wonders that were the cause of awe and amazement. They were signs of who he was and they were accomplished through his human instrumentality. They were extensions of him and his power as the sacraments are now—not *just* signs but efficacious signs, which bring about what they point to.

Now the Eucharist is a sign that points to the Lord as food, in which the sign mysteriously becomes the very reality toward which it points...Jesus Christ in his Body and Blood. Since it is *the* sacrament of sacraments (CCC no. 1330) and the "source and summit of the Christian life" (L.G. 11), it is also called the Blessed Sacrament, especially when reserved in the tabernacle.

St. Thomas Aquinas, in a beautiful passage in the *Summa Theologiae* (S.T. III Q 65, a.3), sees all of the sacraments as pointing to the Eucharist as the center of the Christian life, because it is the sacrament that joins us so closely to the Lord. Baptism and confirmation prepare us for the Eucharist and empower us to lead others to it. Penance restores us to God's friendship so we may receive Communion again after serious sin, and the anointing of the sick restores our health so we may receive again. *Viaticum* is our final Communion. The Lord is with us (*te cum;* literally, with you) on the way *(in via)* to our heavenly homeland beyond the signs of the sacraments. Marriage, which is the sign of the love that Jesus has for the Church, is best seen in the gift of the Eucharist. Celebrating this sacrament is one of the noblest duties of priests and bishops, who are empowered to do so by Holy Orders.

7. Why is the Eucharist called the Divine Liturgy by the churches of the East?

As we have seen the Eucharist may be called "the source and summit of the Christian life" and is so called in *Lumen Gentium* (no. 11), but in *Sacrosanctum Concilium,* the liturgy itself is described as "the summit towards which the activity of the Church is directed…(and) the fount from which all her power flows" (no. 10). The terms *eucharist* and *liturgy* are often used interchangeably, but for the Western Church liturgy is a broader term encompassing the work of the people in all liturgical action. Originally it was a secular Greek term for the work of a citizen or the people for the city-state. In the translation of the Septuagint it was used for the people's worship in the Temple (Numbers) and, later, in the New Testament for the Eucharist (cf. Acts 13:2). Now for the Western Church, *liturgy* refers to the work of Christ on the cross reconciling us to God made present in power in the sacraments and substantially present in the Eucharist and in some way present in the Liturgy of the Hours, the liturgical year, and other ecclesial rites and blessings. When the West speaks of the Eucharist it is referring to the Mass and the reserved Blessed Sacrament, whereas the churches of the East call the Eucharist as celebrated the Divine Liturgy because, as the *Catechism* says "the whole liturgy finds its center and most intense expression in the celebration of this sacrament; in the same sense we also call its celebration the *Sacred Mysteries.*" (no. 1330).

8. Why is the Eucharist called the Breaking of the Bread?

In the accounts of the multiplication of the loaves and fishes, a pattern emerges—the Lord is described as taking the bread, blessing it, breaking it, and giving it (Matt 14:19; 15:36). This is the pattern of the Last Supper (Matt 26:26; 1 Cor 11:24), and this breaking of the bread was how the disciples at Emmaus recognized the Lord (Luke 24:30–31). This became the term that the earliest Christians used to speak of their celebrations of the Eucharist (cf. Acts 2:42, 20:7–11). The breaking of the bread continues at our Mass in the fraction rite during the *Agnus Dei* or "Lamb of God." In fact the basic pattern of Jesus taking the bread, blessing it, breaking it, and giving it is still the shape of our Liturgy of the Eucharist. After the Liturgy of the Word, the priest, representing Christ, "takes the bread" at the preparation of the gifts; he "blesses it" during the recitation of the Eucharistic Prayer, our prayer or blessing and thanksgiving; he "breaks" the host at the fraction; and he "distributes it" at Communion. This fraction reminds us of Christ's Body, which has been broken for us (1 Cor 11:24) and which we receive in the Eucharist, as well as his Word, which has been broken for us in the homily. And so the fathers Jerome and Hilary speak of the two tables of the Word and the Eucharist, as do *The Imitation of Christ* and the great Bossuet in later ages. All point out that the assembly is first nourished by the Word spoken and broken (explained) and then by the eucharistic bread—the one loaf broken for the many (cf. 1 Cor 10:16–17).

9. Why is the Eucharist called Holy Communion?

We hear a great deal today about the Eucharist producing community. It is true that the Eucharist draws Christians closer together, but it is in a communion which is a deeper reality than human community, important as that is. Our communion is with Christ in his Body and Blood (cf. 1 Cor 10:16–17) and makes us into one Body, the Church, united to Christ as our head (cf. 1 Cor

12:12–31; Rom 12:4–8). Our communion with Christ when we receive him in Communion, that is, the Body and Blood of Christ—brings about a deep communion with one another in the "mystical body of Christ," as the Church has been called under this aspect. We have a communitarian or *horizontal* relationship with one another, but it is much more than natural attraction or common interests (which may be lacking) because we are joined together by the *vertical* relationship of all of us to the Father, through Christ and in the Spirit. This is the communion that our Communion of the Body and Blood of Christ brings about in us— with Christ and with one another in him.

_____

THREE

THE STRUCTURE OF THE EUCHARISTIC LITURGY OF THE MASS

10. Why did the Lord use bread and wine?

Bread and wine were common food for Jews at the time that the Lord lived. Even today blessings are said over bread and wine at every Jewish Sabbath meal. Some kind of bread is a staple in most cultures and wine certainly is in that of at least the Mediterranean world. However, there is a much deeper significance to bread and wine on the symbolic level. In Genesis (14:18–21) Abraham is visited by Melchizedek, King of Salem, who offered bread and wine and then disappeared. He was seen as a type of Christ (cf. Heb 7) for the origins of Melchizedek were unknown and those of Christ are mysterious, eternally begotten by the Father before all time and yet incarnate of the Virgin Mary in time. Melchizedek was a priest and king of Salem, and the Lord Jesus is the great High Priest (cf. Heb 9:11) and King of Peace *(shalom)*. Melchizedek offers bread and wine, as does Jesus at the Last Supper, and then disappears, while the Lord, after his resurrection, ascends into heaven.

This is a witness to the custom of the ancients of offering bread and wine, but in the Exodus event, bread figured prominently as well (Exod 12:15). Then the bread did not have time to rise, and so unleavened bread becomes the staple symbol of the Passover meal. In the desert the Israelites were fed by *manna*—a mysterious substance—bread from heaven that God provided for them (Exod 16). Furthermore, ordinary wheaten bread is made from many grains of wheat, and St. Paul will remark on the symbolism of the many grains as representing Christians made one by Christ in his body as grains ground into flour become one in one loaf (1 Cor 10:17). Note that as the wheat must give up its individual grain form, so too, Christians have to give up excessive individualism to be a member of the Church, the Body of Christ, represented by the one loaf.

17

Some of the fathers further saw this flour moistened by the living waters of the Holy Spirit and baked as a loaf in the oven of charity, a symbolism somewhat allegorical, yet rich in meaning. The wine ferments and is "spirited," a symbolizing that both elements will have the Holy Spirit hover over them to become the Body and Blood of Christ.

We have seen the Cup of Blessing of the Passover meal and note that every festive Jewish meal had the cup of wine as a symbol of messianic joy—wine that gladdens the heart of man (Ps 104:15). Finally, note that God is offered in thanksgiving in the Eucharist not just wheat and grapes, but "fruit of the earth," "fruit of the vine," and *"work of human hands,"* and these two gifts of God to us are offered back in thanksgiving representing us, our work, our lives, and all that we are in those words "work of human hands."

11. Must bread and wine still be used?

It is clear from what has been said above that bread and wine were used by the Lord at the Last Supper not simply because they were common food, but also because they were prescribed by the Passover ritual and had deep Jewish roots as well as deep natural and scriptural symbolism. This cannot be changed because the Church judges these material elements to be of the substance or essence of the sacrament. They are the material element or the matter of the sacrament. Because the Lord became flesh in first-century Palestine, born into a Jewish family, that history, that symbolism, that rich tradition, still shapes our sacramental and liturgical life. Therefore the Church insists on wheaten bread, unleavened like Jesus used for the Western Church, and leavened to symbolize the risen Lord for the Eastern Church. For the West, only wheaten flour and water may be used without any additives (cf. Canon 924 and R.S. no. 48). The wine must be natural grape wine with no alcohol added, but can have some sulphates to preserve it (ibid.). Wines from other fruits or rice wines may not be used (R.S. no. 59). Sacramental wines are the safest to use. Mustum is grape juice in which fermentation has begun, but has been suspended with the results that its alcohol content does not reach the level found in most table wines. It can be used by alcoholic priests in celebrating Mass because it is sufficiently fermented grape juice to qualify as wine and yet not so strong as to harm the alcoholic priest. Pasteurized grape juice may not be used because all the alcohol has been evaporated and the nature of the juice is altered, and therefore it would be invalid matter. The local ordinary may give permission for a priest, deacon, or member of the faithful to receive Communion under the form of mustum (cf. *Bishops' Committee on the Liturgy Newsletter,* Nov. 2003). He normally delegates this to the pastor.

12. What if people are allergic to wheat? What if they have celiac sprue disease?

If people are allergic to wheat they can receive the Precious Blood from the chalice, especially if they have celiac sprue disease. This is a disorder causing an allergic intestinal reaction to the gluten in wheat, a protein enzyme that activates when flour is kneaded. Gluten is a toxin to persons with the disease and damages the digestive system, resulting in the prevention of the absorption of vitamins and nutrients, and predisposes its victims to osteoporosis, neurological illnesses, and even lymphoma.

People with this disease can control it by not eating anything containing gluten, which most of their doctors advise. For Catholics this is serious because gluten is contained in communion hosts made only of wheat and water. Such people may receive the Precious Blood from the chalice even if others do not. It can be dangerous for them to drink from the main chalice into which a particle of the host is broken, or even from a cup that has been used for intinction (cf. question 43).

Some advocate low-gluten hosts as the answer to this problem, and permission for such can be given (cf. *Bishops'*

Committee on the Liturgy Newsletter, Nov. 2003); but hosts with *no* gluten are not wheaten and as such fail to possess the required biblical symbolism, as indeed would wafers made from rice or some other substances. The local ordinary may give permission to use low-gluten hosts, and may delegate this to the pastor. Should a sufferer from celiac sprue disease be allergic to low-gluten hosts or not be in a position to obtain such and unable to drink from the chalice, the teaching on spiritual communion, whereby one can receive the grace of the sacrament even if one can't the sacrament itself, can be very consoling.

13. How did the celebration of the Eucharist evolve from the Last Supper?

The Lord told the twelve "to do this in memory of me," and ever since, the Church has celebrated the Eucharist especially on Sunday, the Lord's Day (cf. Acts 20:7; Rev 1:10). At first it would seem they celebrated the Eucharist Saturday evening, because the first Jewish Christians kept the Sabbath as well as Sunday. However, since according to the Jewish reckoning of time each day began at sundown, Saturday evening was the beginning of the Lord's Day. While the Lord celebrated the Eucharist in the context of the Passover, that ritual was only for that once-a-year feast. However, there was another ritual meal form, the *chaburah,* or friendship meal, that had a blessing and distribution of bread at its beginning and a solemn blessing over the Cup of Blessing at the end, as did the Sabbath meal. This form of the eucharistic celebration, including a meal alongside the eucharistic elements, is attested to in the *Didache* and in St. Paul's complaint about selfishness and drunkenness in the eucharistic celebration of the Corinthian church (1 Cor 11:20–23). As the number of Christians increased (through St. Paul's missionary journeys more and more Gentiles came into the Church), there were simply too many to continue the meal as a part of the Eucharist. The prayer over the elements of bread and wine that had become the Body and Blood of Christ was the essential reality, and all knew that this was the core of the Eucharist. Sometimes an *agapé* or fellowship meal was still celebrated in the evening, because as the Church moved more and more into the Gentile world, where there was no Sabbath observance and Sunday was just a workday, the celebration of the Eucharist took place early in the morning. Pliny the Younger, writing to Trajan the emperor, reports on the Christians singing hymns to Christ as God at sunup, and this is commonly understood to be the celebration of the Eucharist.

We have two descriptions of the Liturgy of the Eucharist in the apology of St. Justin (Apology I, 65–66), a document written to explain the behavior of Christians to the emperor (c. 155). He describes the baptism of converts and then goes on to explain how bread and wine are brought forth to the one presiding and that he prays a Eucharistic Prayer "as well as he can" letting us know that it was prayed extemporaneously then but using certain broad well-known themes. St. Hippolytus, fifty years later, offers a Eucharistic Prayer as a model for use or copying, and it is the basis of Eucharistic Prayer II for us in the Roman Rite. To return to St. Justin, he concludes by describing communion of the "eucharisted" or consecrated bread and wine by all and deacons taking it to the absent. By the year 200 or so the basic structure of the Liturgy of the Eucharist is essentially set.

14. Why does the Church celebrate the Eucharist on Sunday?

The simple answer is because it is the day that the Lord rose from the dead, and each Sunday is like a little Easter, a memorial of the first Easter. However, there are many more themes and reasons, and John Paul II explored the many facets of this question in *Dies Domini,* "The Day of the Lord."

For us, Sunday is "the day the LORD has made," in which we rejoice and are glad (Ps 118:24). Its foundation is the Jewish Sabbath, which is a reflection of the Lord's resting in the Book of Genesis after creating the world in six days (Gen 2:2). Our Jewish brethren celebrate the Sabbath on Saturday even to this day. I once took my class to an Orthodox synagogue for the evening service, which was mostly chanted by the men in Hebrew. However, it was Friday evening—the beginning of the Sabbath—and for the benefit of my class, they sang one song in English: a hauntingly beautiful one welcoming the Sabbath as a lovely bride. Such was their joy on beginning the day of rest, the day of prayer, the day of ritual, the day of family.

Since the Lord rose on the first day of the week, the celebration of the Eucharist, in which the early Christians experienced the risen Lord with them, Sunday was chosen as the day of worship and of the Eucharist. The apostles felt free to make such a change, although some early Christians celebrated both the Sabbath and Sunday. This has given rise to the hypothesis that the first Jewish Christians kept the Sabbath with their Jewish brethren and then on the Sabbath evening (the beginning of the first day of the week) celebrated the Eucharist among themselves after sundown. In any event, the New Testament is replete with references to gatherings for "the breaking of the bread" on the first day of the week, for example, at Troas, where St. Paul restored a boy to life (Acts 20:7–12) or in Corinth, where a collection for Paul's support was recommended (1 Cor 16:2). Pliny the Younger, governor of Bithynia, speaks of Christians gathering on a set day early in the morning and singing "a hymn to Christ as a god" (D.D., no. 21). As Christianity moved into the pagan world, their observance of worship on the first day of the week would not have been respected, for Sunday was a workday. Whereas the Jewish day began at sundown, the Roman day commenced at sunrise. Therefore, in pagan society Christians gathered before sunrise on the first day of the week, as Pliny bears witness. It was only in the fourth century that civil and ecclesiastical law forbade servile work on that day.

Such fathers of the Church as St. Ignatius of Antioch, St. Justin, St. Augustine, and St. Isidore of Seville all give a rationale for transferring the Sabbath to Sunday, and the later fathers, for

Sabbath rest on that day as well. For as St. Gregory the Great declares, "For us, the true Sabbath is the person of our redeemer, our Lord Jesus Christ" (Epistle 13:1).

Sunday is not only a little Easter, as we have seen and St. Basil attests: "...holy Sunday, honored by the Lord's Resurrection, the first fruits of all the other days" (Homilies in Hexaemeron II; 8). The Sabbath was God's "day of rest" after the work of creation, and Sunday is dedicated to the work of the new creation in Christ's saving death and resurrection. The fathers saw it as the first day of the *new* week, thus counting the six days of creation, the Sabbath, and Sunday, thus making it the eighth day—the day of eternity. As St. Basil states, it is "the day without end which will know neither evening nor morning" (On the Holy Spirit, 27, 66). This is the reason that many baptisteries were octagonal in the early Church, because in them one was born into eternal life. As the day of the sun, Sunday seems to have been a day of pagan worship of the sun, wisely reinterpreted as a day celebrating Christ, the Light of the World, to draw the faithful from pagan cults (D.D., no. 27). Since the Spirit was given on Pentecost Sunday, Sunday is also seen as the day of the Spirit (John 20:22–23). St. Thomas the apostle's doubt turned to faith on Sunday (John 20:27–29).

All of these themes are richly explored in John Paul's *Dies Domini,* and give a convincing rationale for our celebration of the Eucharist on Sunday.

15. How did the Liturgy of the Word come to be?

The Jewish Christians had kept going to the Temple (cf. Acts 3:1) and the synagogue for prayers, and they would listen to the Law and the prophets and would understand them as pertaining to Jesus, the new Moses and the last and greatest of the prophets. As the Church moved into the Gentile world, celebrating the Eucharist early in the morning, without the meal itself, and as Jewish converts missed the Hebrew reading, a Christian form of synagogal worship began to develop. We now call this the Liturgy of the Word. Whereas the Jews listened to the Law and the prophets, listened to the rabbi's explanation and prayed for Israel; now Christians listened to the prophets, followed by the Gospels or "memoirs of the apostles," as St. Justin calls them (Apology I, 65–67). He further explains how then they listened to the explanation given by the one who is presiding (most likely a bishop at this time) and that all would rise and pray for themselves and for all in need of prayer. As the Letters of Paul were collected, they got added to the reading, and so the first part of the Mass as it evolved structurally is roughly the same as that which we use today, although different ceremonial details have been added on or eliminated.

16. Why is the Mass celebrated in different rites?

We have seen how the eucharistic liturgy evolved from the Christian *chaburah* form to that of Sts. Justin and Hippolytus as well as how the synagogal liturgy became the Liturgy of the Word. When Egeria, a Spanish pilgrim to the Holy Land in the fourth century, described the Palm Sunday celebration in Jerusalem, her only comment is that it is the "same as elsewhere." Since she wrote from Jerusalem, came from Spain, and stopped at many ports en route where, as a devout pilgrim, she would have participated in the Eucharist, this is a telling comment. The basic structure of the Eucharist was quasi-universal, and yet while the format of the Mass or the Divine Liturgy was established, it was embellished ceremonially differently in those different cultures and thus the origins of different rites came about. Among these rites are the Armenian, Byzantine, Chaldean, Coptic, Ethiopian, Maronite, Syrian, and many more, enriching the Eucharist with different emphases on different aspects of the great mystery, but at core the same divine reality.

Although we can see here the beginnings of enculturation, of incarnating the essential core of Gospel, liturgy, and Eucharist into the legitimate cultures of those newly evangelized, not every-thing was changed. Many Christians enjoy singing *alleluia, hosanna,* and *amen* without knowing that these Hebrew words mean "praise God," "acclaim God, our Helper," and "so be it" respectively, and the fact that these Hebrew words were not incul-turated seems to bother very few.

17. What is an Eastern-Rite liturgy like?

As we have seen, there are many rites in the Catholic Church, many Eastern rites. I shall describe only the Byzantine Rite, which is used by the Albanians, Bulgarians, Carpatho-Russians, Greeks, Melchites, Slovakians, Russians, Ukrainians, and the vast majority of Orthodox Christians. Its origin seems to be from Palestine, Antioch, and Cappadocia, and was transformed by St. Basil the Great and St. John Chrysostom. It developed and flourished in the new capital of the empire, Constantinople, which was named for the first Christian emperor, Constantine.

As the empire became more Eastern and separated from the West, it was called Byzantium. This name came to describe the rite celebrated throughout the Eastern Empire—Byzantine.

The Divine Liturgy begins with a preparation rite behind the icon screen or Iconostasis. After the priest and deacon vest, they prepare the gifts at a side altar—a loaf of leavened bread and wine. The loaf is cut in certain particles and arranged symboli-cally on the paten. The elements and coverings are incensed and the deacon goes to incense altar, icons, and people.

The priest begins the liturgy by blessing himself with the Gospel Book, and the deacon leads the faithful in a litany (prayer of the faithful). After each petition, the response is, "Lord have mercy." At the Little Entrance, the Gospel Book is carried in with great solemnity. The deacon sings, "Wisdom, let us stand erect," as the Gospel Book is placed on the altar. After two antiphons are chanted, the *Trisagion* is chanted as well: "Holy God, Holy Mighty One, Holy Immortal One, have mercy on us." The lector chants one Epistle, the deacon chants the Gospel, and the homily is given, although sometimes it is postponed until the end. After litanies, the cherubic hymn is sung and the Great Entrance follows, in which the priest, carrying the elements of bread and wine before the people and blessing them, goes to the altar through the central (or royal) doors of the Iconostasis. After more litanies, the Creed is chanted, the Preface is begun, and the choir responds with the *Sanctus*. After a short prayer of thanksgiving, the priest sings the Words of Institution and all respond "Amen." The *Epiclesis* follows, and while the priest continues with the canon, litanies are sung by the deacon and the people, concluding with the Our Father. The priest offers the gifts to the faithful: "Holy things for the holy." Then the consecrated bread is further broken into four pieces, one of which is placed in the chalice, while the others are cut into small particles for Holy Communion and placed in the consecrated wine. The faithful are invited to "approach with faith and in the fear of God," and they receive both species from a little golden spoon dipped into the chalice. Hymns and litanies are sung, and after a prayer before the Iconostasis, the priest gives the blessing with the final prayer, and then gives the cross of blessing to the faithful to be kissed while the deacon consumes any remaining Communion.

18. What is the priest's role in the Eucharist?

The *Catechism of the Catholic Church* sees the celebration of the liturgy as an "action" of the whole Christ (*Christus totus* no. 1136). This Eucharist or thanksgiving to the Father is offered through Christ, the great high priest, in the power of the Holy Spirit. It is a celebration of the mystical body of Christ, the Church, but an ordered celebration, and the one presiding is normally the priest. The Lord presided at the Last Supper and presided from the cross at the great timeless eternal sacrifice. He told the twelve "to do this in memory of me," and the apostles knew he meant that they were to celebrate the supper of the

Lord's Body "given for you" (Luke 22:19; cf. also Mark 14:22 and Matt 26:26) and Blood "poured out for you" (Mark 14:23; Matt 26:28). Indeed, St. Paul is very clear to hand on the tradition:

> ...I received from the Lord what I also handed on to you...the Lord Jesus...took...bread...and said, "This is my body that is for you."...In the same way he took the cup also,...saying "This cup is the new covenant in my blood. Do this, as often as you drink it, in remembrance of me." (1 Cor 11:23–26)

It is clear that not just anyone could preside at the eucharistic celebration, but only the apostles or one appointed by them. The one presiding represents Christ, acts *in persona Christi capitis*—in the person of Christ the Head (cf. 2 Cor 2:10). The ordinary celebrant in the early Church was the bishop as the successor of the apostles. Indeed, St. Ignatius was very clear about this: "Let only that Eucharist be regarded as legitimate, which is celebrated under the bishop or him to whom he has entrusted it (*Ad Smyrna* 8:1). We also see in Ignatius that the bishop could entrust it to another, namely one of the *presbyters* or priests of the second rank who are mentioned in the Pastoral Epistles and who began assisting the bishops by celebrating in their stead, especially in rural areas.

It is clear that the tradition of the Church is that only a bishop or a priest can represent Christ, the great High Priest and Head of the Body—to act *in persona Christi capitis*. (CCC no. 1348). The reason is that the Eucharist is a celebration of the whole Church. Not just anyone can preside, for not all Christians have the power to do so. The one who represents Christ must have his power passed on from the apostles, who received it from him: "Do this in memory of me." Thus the priest acts for the Church with the authority of Christ, the Head of the Body, and not his own. This is the meaning of his acting *in persona Christi capitis*. "The priest who presides at the celebration, however, always retains the right of arranging those things that are his responsibility" (GIRM no. 111), so that "there should be harmony and diligence in the effective preparation of each liturgical celebration in accord with the Missal and other liturgical books" (ibid.). All "whether they are ordained ministers or lay Christian faithful, in fulfilling their office or their duty, should carry out solely but completely that which pertains to them" (ibid., no. 91).

19. Why can't a woman preside as a priest?

The Church teaches clearly the equality of men and women, and indeed John Paul II taught in *Mulieris Dignitatem* that in the act of procreation, woman is greater than man, who in some way stands outside the mystery of the new life growing within her. While in a way *he* began that life in his contribution of the seed, yet *she* gives much more from her very being than he, and therefore is greater in that way (M.D. 18).

The question is answered by tradition, which is a source of the Catholic faith along with the Scriptures, the former interpreting the latter and passing on the Gospel. Before the New Testament was written, the Gospel was passed on in preaching and celebration, and later was written down. In the seventies, in the era of ecumenical progress, seeing that other Christian bodies had women ministers (although this was not true of the Eastern Orthodox), Catholic theologians began to question if women could be ordained priests. The Biblical Commission could find nothing in Scripture against the practice, so Pope Paul VI referred the matter to the Congregation of the Doctrine of the Faith in 1975. The CDF, however, found scriptural reasons why this could not be done, but based its arguments primarily on tradition—that the Church, whether East or West, has never done this or thought of it, whereas heretical groups in the early Church had done so.

The document of the CDF, *Inter Insignores* (1976), pointed out that at the Last Supper there were only the Twelve, not even the Blessed Virgin, when the Lord said, "Do this in remembrance of me." St. Paul, who worked with women, who called them his fellow workers in the mission of evangelization, never called them God's coworkers (I.I. no. 3), a term he restricted to pastors. He does single out Junias, which could be a feminine name, or far more likely a masculine name in the feminine form, not that uncommon in Latin and Greek. It is true that the word *presbytera* appears in the tradition, but it seems to mean priest's wife. It is true that there were deaconesses in the early Church, but they were not considered ordained, and their work was primarily to aid in the baptism of nude adult women catechumens and minister to the women afterward. As infant baptism became the norm, their liturgical work ceased, and that of charity and ministry to women was taken over more by women monastics as that movement made its influence felt in the Church. In the East deaconesses were "ordained" but *not* at the altar and not for the service of the altar.

John Paul II underscored the teaching of *Inter Insignores* in 1996, when he issued *Ordinatio Sacerdotalis,* in which he stated the Church holds that she cannot ordain women. He did not explicate the reasons, but let those enunciated previously stand. It seems to me that the tradition is based on Christian anthropology and not simply social roles at the time of the Lord. In fact *Inter Insignores* states that (no. 4) and John Paul II underscored it in M.D. when he said that the Lord was sovereignly free in going against many of the customs of his time, especially in the attention he gave women, but he did not call them to be among the Twelve, not even his mother (no. 26). Could it be that the complementarity of man and woman in the order of nature is also found in the order of the supernatural?

We have seen how the priest acts *in persona Christi capitis* at Mass; he represents Christ at the altar. The East would call him an icon of Christ. *Inter Insignores,* quoting St. Thomas, points out that in a sign or a symbol there needs to be likeness between the sign and the reality it signifies (no. 5). This would mean that if the priest is to represent Christ, the Man-God, then that likeness must include his gender. Perhaps if the priest were a sign of God in general (since God is pure Spirit) it might be a different story, but since the Incarnation means that the Word was embodied in the male form, then the one representing him must be male as well. Some see this as discrimination against women, but no one, man or woman, has a right to ordination. If one is to use the language of rights, one could argue that a male virgin is discriminated against because only women can be consecrated virgins! Actually only a man can represent Christ and the Father as well because he is not only the *sign* of Christ, but the *only* adequate sign of the Father. Procreation begins with the father, as creation begins with our heavenly Father, and the priest represents the Father as well as acting *in persona Christi capitis*. Women cannot in their bodies and being represent that reality.

On the other hand, men cannot represent the Virgin Mother Church the way a woman can, which is why men cannot be consecrated virgins. They cannot be the sign of Mother Church bringing to birth from the "womb" of the baptismal font new neophytes or children for God. They cannot represent Mother Church (a patristic image based on Gal 4:26–27) giving the pure milk of spiritual teaching (1 Cor 3:2), because only a woman's body is the beautiful sign of the Virgin Mother Church. There is then a complementarity between the sexes, making them different though equal. Only a man can be a father and only a woman can be a mother. A man represents Christ and the Father, whether as a priest or as husband and father, though as a Christian he is in the Church; and only a woman can represent the Virgin Mother Church, whether as a consecrated virgin (or religious) or a wife and mother, even though as a Christian, she is in Christ. Complementarity is a gift naturally; the supernatural order builds on, rather than destroys, this substratum.

Von Balthasar would contrast the Marian (or female) principle to the Petrine (or male) principle. When the male principle dominates in the Church (necessary as it is) one has "organizations, advisory commissions, academies, parties, pressure groups, functions, structures and restructurings, sociological experiments, statistics" (*Elucidations,* p. 110). Our Lady under the cross represented the Church and is given to us, represented by John, as mother. Her maternal mothering role can only be fulfilled in the Church by women who make that utterly self-giving contribution in the Church in their *being* more than in their *doing*. Men fulfill the Petrine structural roles, whether ruling as Peter, preaching as Paul, or representing priesthood as John.

Finally, we are speaking of the authority of the Church, which is not absolute. It must base its teaching and practice on the authority of God's revelation in Scripture and tradition. The Church cannot authorize what it believes God has not authorized, as John Paul II pointed out in *Ordinatio Sacerdotalis.*

20. Is there a difference between how the priest offers and how the laity offer this sacrifice?

In *Lumen Gentium* the council fathers clearly state that "though they differ essentially and not only in degree, the common priesthood of the faithful and the ministerial or hierarchical priesthood are nonetheless ordered to one another; each in its own proper way shares in the one priesthood of Christ" (L.G. no. 10).

This means that for Christians there is only one priesthood, that of Jesus Christ, the great High Priest (Heb 9:11). Just as Israel of old was God's holy priestly people (Exod 19:6), so Christians are "a chosen race, a royal priesthood, a holy nation, God's own people" (1 Pet 2:9, 4–5), and yet this priesthood is structured into the hierarchical or ministerial, which ministers to or serves that royal priesthood of all the faithful. This ministerial priesthood "forms and rules the priestly people; *in persona Christi,* (and) effects the eucharistic sacrifice and offers it to God in the name of all the people" (L.G. no. 10) and "the only minister who can confect the sacrament of the Eucharist…is a validly ordained priest" (R.S. no. 146). The faithful, in turn "by virtue of their royal priesthood, participate in the offering of the Eucharist…exercise that priesthood in the reception of the sacraments, prayer and thanksgiving, the witness of a holy life, abnegation, and active charity" (ibid.). They offer their "bodies as a living sacrifice, holy and acceptable to God, which is your spiritual worship" (Rom 12:2). The Decree on the Apostolate of Lay People recognizes that the particular gift of lay people is to penetrate the secular sphere with the Gospel (no. 5), and *Gaudium et Spes* of Vatican II and *Christifideles Laici* of John Paul II do the same. Their prayer of intercession, whether at Mass, the Liturgy of the Hours, or individually, is an exercise of their baptismal priesthood that immensely benefits the whole Church (cf. GIRM, no. 69).

21. Are there other roles in the liturgy?

St. Paul very well describes the Church as the Body of Christ with the many different roles in the body (cf. 1 Cor 12:12 et seq.) and the fathers of the Church saw the Church in the same way, especially in celebrating the Eucharist. The many different liturgical roles complemented one another and were not in competition. In the local church the whole Church was represented by the bishop, representing Christ as well and in union with the successor of Peter, the bishop of Rome, and therefore in communion with the whole Church. He was surrounded by his presbyters or priests who assisted him, by his deacons who distributed Communion, by the lectors who read, by the singers in the *schola cantorum* who led the singing, by the people who brought forth the gifts and prayed and received Communion. Often the virgins had a special place of honor in the assembly. The local church in union with the whole Church as the *totus Christus,* the whole Christ as a priestly people, were all celebrating according to his or her role, all offering themselves and their lives in union with Christ's sacrifice according to their state in life.

This is true today, with the priest presiding over the celebration, preaching and saying the Eucharistic Prayer, within which the consecration takes place (cf. R.S. no. 146). Other priests sometimes concelebrate (in the proper sense) with him, and deacons may assist in proclaiming the Gospel and helping to distribute Communion. Lectors read; their role is ministerial and therefore not to be usurped by the priest presiding (cf. GIRM no. 59). Leaders of song, cantors, and choirs help us with the music, and designated acolytes or ministers of the Eucharist help distribute Communion when there is need. When the laity offer the intercessions, the GIRM sees them as exercising their baptismal priesthood (no. 69). Ushers and greeters keep order in the assembly so all can participate in listening, praying, singing, offering, and communing. Christ's priestly people offer themselves with and through the priest, receive him in his Body in return, and become more his Body, the Church, at prayer.

22. What are the parts of the Eucharistic Prayer?

We have seen how the Eucharistic Prayer derives from the Jewish *berakah* prayer of praise, blessing, and thanksgiving. We have seen how the earliest ones from apostolic times on seem to have been extempore but based on certain broad themes. These themes began to be set down and codified and we have texts from the *Didache* (c. 100), St. Hippolytus (c. 215), the Apostolic Constitutions (fourth century), St. Basil (fourth century), and the Roman Canon (c. 300), etcetera. Although some of these prayers are more Western (Alexandrian) and some more Eastern (Antiochene), we can see certain common elements that are found in all Eucharistic Prayers, sometimes called an anaphora from the Greek "lifting on high," as indeed the gifts are by this prayer. The elements are:

The *Preface:* As the Jews praised God for the Exodus of old, Christians praised God for their Exodus from the slavery of sin into the new life of grace accomplished through the death and resurrection of Christ. The Preface gives the particular motives for thanks, singling out different moments of salvation history or summing them all up as does Eucharistic Prayer IV. The Preface concludes with the *Sanctus,* the song of the angels to the thrice holy God from Isaiah 6, mentioned by Pope St. Clement in his letters as a Christian liturgical chant. The "Holy, holy, holy" reminds us that our liturgy is cosmic, and in it, heaven and earth join in praising God.

The *Epiclesis:* After a transition from the *Sanctus,* this prayer calls down (*epi klao* in Greek) the Holy Spirit to change the bread and wine into the Body and Blood of Christ. Another *Epiclesis* after the Consecration calls down the Spirit on the Assembly so that those who eat the Body of the Lord and drink his Blood might become one in him.

The *Institution Narrative:* Traditionally also called the Consecration, the words of institution said by the Lord at the Last Supper, "This is my Body," "This is my Blood," are said by the priest in the name of Christ and in the power of the Spirit, and so change the bread and wine into the Body and Blood of Christ.

The *Anamnesis* or memorial follows in which the Church commemorates the saving death and resurrection and return of our Lord and Savior Jesus Christ, which mystery is now present and which the Church offers, priest and people, to the Father in the unity and power of the Holy Spirit.

The *Intercessions* or commemorations now take place. The assembly prays in union with the whole Church of heaven, with Our Lady, all the saints and angels and in union with and for the whole Church on earth, the pope, our local bishop and clergy, for all of the faithful of the Church universal, and for all people of good will, as well as for the dead.

The *Great Amen* concludes the Eucharistic Prayer. It is our assent, our agreement to the great prayer the priest (or bishop) has said for us in the name of the whole Church. That is his role, and ours to respond that we accept this prayer as our own as it is offered to the Father through his Son: "Through him, with him, in him in the unity of the Holy Spirit all glory and honor is yours almighty Father, for ever and ever." St. Justin tells us that *amen* is a Hebrew word that means "so be it" (Apology I, 65) and it is attributed to St. Jerome that, when he heard the Great Amen sung in the basilicas of Rome, it seemed to him that it sounded like a "mighty thunder."

23. Why do we have so many Eucharistic Prayers?

For centuries the Roman Canon (Eucharistic Prayer I) was the only prayer in the Roman Rite. After Vatican II, when the liturgy was being officially reformed, many liturgists asked to have some other possibilities, either some of the great Eucharistic Prayers from other liturgical traditions or new ones modeled after ancient prayers, such as those of Sts. Basil, James, John Chrysostom, and others. So other prayers were added to the first Eucharistic Prayer. Now we have:

Eucharistic Prayer I or the Roman Canon: This prayer is mentioned by St. Ambrose in his *De Sacramentis* and is therefore very ancient. It is in the Alexandrian tradition of having intercession before and after the Words of Institution. It is Roman in its sobriety, its gravity, and its lists of Roman martyrs or those saints who were popular with the Roman people. This prayer heavily emphasizes the sacrificial dimensions of the Eucharist. It is recommended for special seasons and occasions, especially when there are proper parts.

Eucharistic Prayer II: This is basically the Eucharistic Prayer that St. Hippolytus (c. 215) composed as a model for others. It is brief and concise, and since it was edited for contemporary usage, the *Sanctus* was added because the original text was bereft of that acclamation. Also, as the early Church was being led to deeper understanding as to the ramifications of who Christ was, the Holy Spirit helped to crystallize formulas that were precise. The text of St. Hippolytus lacked some of that precision and seemed a bit Adoptionist, and that lack was corrected in our contemporary text. This prayer is designed for daily use.

Eucharistic Prayer III: This is a contemporary composition in the light of ancient variants from the Galliean and Hispanic traditions. This prayer is recommended for Sundays and funerals (because of the special part for the dead.)

Eucharistic Prayer IV: This prayer is modeled after that of St. Basil, who recounted all of salvation history in his prayer. This does the same (though not in as great detail as did he) both before and after the *Sanctus*. When first issued, it was recommended for those with the biblical culture to understand it, but that no longer seems to be the case. It's probably too long pastorally to be used in parishes for daily Mass. It is that prayer in the Roman Rite that helps us to breathe "with both lungs" as Pope John Paul would have had us Latins do.

Two prayers of reconciliation were introduced under Pope Paul VI for the Holy Year of 1975. They are appropriate during Lent, times of war or strife, or when prayers for unity are called for. Three prayers for Masses with children use a simpler style of language while trying to avoid the childish and yet bringing the children's participation in more to capture and hold their attention.

The four Eucharistic Prayers for Various Needs and Occasions have four different themes: the Church on the way to unity, God guides the Church on the way to salvation, Jesus the way to the Father, and Jesus the Compassion of God. The *Roman Missal* suggests occasions when these prayers would be appropriate.

FOUR

THE SACRIFICE OF THE MASS

24. What does *anamnesis* mean, and how does it relate to the Mass as sacrifice?

The Church has always held *that* the Mass is a sacrifice but never precisely defined *how* this is true. We need to understand *memorial* or *anamnesis,* to use the Greek word, or *zakar,* to use the Hebrew term. When the Hebrews celebrated Passover or another feast commemorating a past event, they did not see the past only as dead history, but an event that was still real or "present" now. Something of the Exodus event is made present in each Passover celebration as a sign now and for the future. They thought God was with them in fleeing Egypt, passing through the desert and bringing them to the Promised Land; so was he with them now, delivering them, and would be in the future. A Jewish Rabbi once said to me "Father, every Jewish child is born 3000 years old," meaning that Jewish history, which is "alive", is that child's story as well. The Lord Jesus was a Jew, taught well by the Jewish Joseph and Miriam, and at the Last Supper when he said, "Do this in memory of me" or "as a memorial," he didn't just mean, "When you do this, think of me." Rather, since the events of Holy Thursday were in anticipation of Good Friday, "my blood which *will be shed"* [italics added] and Good Friday can only be understood in the light of the resurrection on the "third day." The Lord thereby established a sacrificial meal that would represent the mystery of the cross (his death and resurrection), and would make it "present," just as the memorial meal of the Exodus had done for the Jews. St. Paul recognizes this: "For as often as you eat this bread and drink the cup, you proclaim the Lord's death until he comes" (1 Cor 11:26). He intended his presence in this mystery under the signs of bread and wine that become him in his Body and Blood, that is, the whole person. The risen Lord in his death and resurrection is made present now for us. As the GIRM says of this anamnesis or memorial: "In fulfillment of the command received from Christ the Lord through the apostles, the Church keeps his memorial by recalling especially his passion, resurrection and ascension" (no. 79e). John Paul II, in *Ecclesia de Eucharistia,* wrote that all of the events of the Triduum "embrace the *mysterium paschale* (the paschal mystery). They also embrace the *mysterium eucharisticum* (the eucharistic mystery)" (no. 2).

Therefore, on the next day, when Jesus offered himself as a total sacrifice, as a holocaust, to the Father, as the new Adam who died an obedient death on the tree of the cross, he undid what the old Adam had done at the behest of Eve, seduced by the serpent, eating the forbidden fruit of the tree of knowledge of good and evil (Gen 3:6). In this bloody sacrifice of Christ, offered "once and for all" (cf. Heb 7:27), the Church "commemorates Christ's Passover and it is made present: the sacrifice Christ offered...on the Cross remains ever present" (CCC no. 1364).

The *Didache* calls the Eucharist a sacrifice (no. 14) as do the fathers of the Church: Sts. Cyril of Jerusalem, Ambrose, Augustine, and many others gradually came to a deeper awareness of the sacrificial nature of the liturgy. Let us give the last word to St. Augustine as he describes participation of the whole City of God in this sacrifice:

> This wholly redeemed city and society of the saints is offered to God as a universal sacrifice by the priest, who in the form of a slave went so far as to offer himself for us in his passion, to make us the Body of so great a head....Such is the sacrifice of Christians "we who are one Body in Christ" (Rom 12:5). The Church continues to reproduce this sacrifice in the sacrament of the altar so well known to believers and it is evident to them that in what she offers, she herself is offered. City of God (10, 6)

25. Does the sacrifice of the Mass add to the sacrifice of the cross?

This was very much a Protestant preoccupation and one that still bothers fundamentalists today. It is interesting to note that St. Thomas in his *Summa* devotes three very long questions to the treatment of Christ's presence in the Eucharist (S.T. III, qq 75–77), and devotes only one very brief article in the question on the "Rite of this Sacrament" (S.T. III, q 83, a.4) to the question as to "Whether Christ is sacrificed in this Sacrament." His answer is that on the cross he was offered up, and that sacrifice was capable of giving salvation, and we offer that same sacrifice each day in memory of his death, quoting St. Ambrose. That this memory is a living memorial for him is clear when quotes an ancient collect to the effect that "whenever the commemoration of this sacrifice is celebrated, the work of our redemption is enacted" (cf. also CCC no. 1364 and L.G. no. 3).

Further, he would see Christ as priest immolating himself (giving himself completely as victim) in this sacrifice as he did on the cross. Thomists see it as specifically and numerically the same sacrifice. Only the manner of offering is different. The *Catechism* quotes Trent to the effect that in the Mass "the same Christ who offered himself once in a bloody manner on the altar of the cross is contained and is offered in an unbloody manner" (CCC no. 1367; Council of Trent [1562]; D.S. 1743). This is true because as we have pointed out before, the nature of the eucharistic memorial in which "the sacrifice Christ offered once and for all on the Cross remains ever present." The Reformers were troubled by the "once and for all" nature of the sacrifice of the cross stressed by the author of the Letter to the Hebrews (7:27). They thought Catholic teaching meant each Mass added another sacrifice to the one all-sufficient sacrifice of the all perfect Man-God, which was (and is) infinite. Such a teaching would be blasphemy, but although certain trends in sixteenth-century Catholic theology may have tended in that direction, such was not, nor is not, the teaching of the Church, as we have explained. Luther further objected that this would make each Mass a "work" we were doing rather than a benefit from God flowing from his Son's work on the cross, but the only reason the Eucharist is celebrated again and again (even daily) in time, is so that we can enter in and accept here and now as a Church (as the Lord's Body) the sacrifice, that all-sufficient work of sacrifice he offered and accomplished "once and for all." This sacrifice exists in the eternity of Christ's divinity, but we need it to be applied to us in time, where we exist now. And so Mass is celebrated again and again, so we can enter in and offer ourselves in union with him. Many Protestant theologians are now more open to the Jewish understanding of "memorial" and what it might mean for the Eucharist.

John Paul II wrote in *Ecclesia de Eucharistia* that, so decisive is the sacrifice of the cross for the salvation of the human race, that Christ "offered it and returned to the Father, only *after he had left a means of sharing in it* as if we were there" (no. 11). This means that the Mass, a *sacrifice in a strict sense* (no. 13), applies to men and women today the reconciliation won once and for all by Christ for mankind in every age (no. 12). The Mass does not add to the sacrifice, nor does it multiply it; the sacrifice of Christ (on the cross) and the sacrifice of the Eucharist are one single sacrifice. What is repeated is the memorial celebration—its *memorialis demonstratio* (commemorative representation) (no. 12). What happened once on the cross is represented (made present) for us here and now. *Redemptionis Sacramentum* stresses that the Eucharist, while a sacred meal, is primarily and "preeminently" a sacrifice (no. 38).

26. Didn't the Old Rite (Tridentine Mass) better exhibit the sacrificial nature of the Mass?

Many hold this position, and it may be somewhat true, but it is clear from what has been said above that the Church clearly understands the Mass as a sacrifice. When this was contested at the time of the Reformation, certain theories of sacrifice grew up identifying the offering of the victim with the Offertory of the Mass, the acceptance of the victim with the Consecration, and the destruction of the victim with Communion. Older readers might remember this particularly in terms of the moral and legal question: How late could one arrive at Mass and not have to attend another? The strict answer was the Gospel, and the less strict was the Offertory, because that was thought to be when the sacrifice was said to begin. Today most liturgists would say in answer to this query: One ought to be there for most of the Liturgy of the Word. To get back to the Mass of the 1962 *Missal,* the language of the Offertory was very sacrificial and in fact the prayer *Suspice sancta Trinitas,* "Receive, O Holy Trinity" (originally "Holy Father") seemed to some liturgists as if it were a "little canon" already offering the sacrifice before the Words of Institution. When I was a child I remember thinking how could Jesus be offered up if he wasn't here yet. I didn't know that much eucharistic language in many rites is anticipatorily sacrificial and that in liturgy one is on the level of the timeless and eternal anyhow. In any event the reform of the Mass after the council removed this "little canon" and substituted two Christianized Jewish prayers of *berakah* or blessing and thanksgiving that we have discussed elsewhere.

The old-rite liturgy always used the ancient Roman Canon, whose language was rich in sacrificial allusions, especially in terms of Old Testament types. The word *sacrifice* appeared frequently throughout the liturgical rite. Today most sacramental theologians would hold that the sacrifice is to be found in the Consecration or Words of Institution when the elements of bread and wine, which have been set aside in the preparation of the gifts, now become the Body and Blood of the risen Lord, who gave himself in sacrifice to the Father on the cross in a bloody way and now gives himself to the Father under the signs, and to us as well, because these signs become our food and drink, the Body and Blood of Christ.

Because of the change of the Offertory prayers, the introduction of new Eucharistic Prayers, whose sacrificial language was less liturgical, and because there were Protestant observers at the Vatican Council, whose forebears clearly did not hold to the sacrificial nature of the Eucharist, some thought the Mass as promulgated by the *Missal* of Paul VI was not the Mass, was no longer a sacrifice, but a Protestant communion service. Interestingly enough, Archbishop Lefebvre, though he did not approve of the "new Mass," did not hold this view. The General Instruction of the Roman Missal issued by Paul VI emphasized that the Mass was and continued to be a sacrifice.

John Paul II encouraged bishops to be generous in allowing the Tridentine Mass to be celebrated for those Catholics still attached to this form, with the stipulation that they need to recognize the validity (essential reality) of the current Mass as the same as the old Mass at core, even though ceremonially there were many differences. Increasingly, there are churches where the Old-Rite Mass is offered using the 1962 *Missal* with the bishop's permission, which are not the chapels of the followers of the deceased Archbishop Lefebvre.

FIVE

CHRIST'S PRESENCE IN THE EUCHARIST

27. How is Christ present in the eucharistic liturgy?

Sacrosanctum Concilium (no. 7) speaks of Christ's presence in the assembly gathered, citing Matthew 18:20: "For where two or three are gathered in my name, I am there among them." We have seen the background of the Liturgy of the Word and how it evolved from the synagogue service. The rabbis taught wherever ten good Jews listened to the Word of God in the Torah, then God would be with them. Jesus takes this tradition of the *minyan* and reduces the number from ten to two or three, and says *he* will be there when Christians gather. So we see the presence of the Lord in the assembly or community and in the Word proclaimed, "...since it is he himself who speaks when the holy scriptures are read in the church." We have seen how the priest presides *in persona Christi capitis,* and *Sacrosanctum Concilium* stresses that Christ is present "in the person of his minister" as well. He is present in all of the sacraments, "so that when anybody baptizes it is really Christ himself who baptizes" (St. Augustine: *Treatise on John,* Bk VI, ch 1, no. 7, quoted in S.C. #7), and finally in the eucharistic species of his Body and Blood, which "is called 'Real' not as a way of excluding all other types of presence as if they were 'not real' but because it is presence in the fullest sense" (M.F. no. 39).

I like to think of these modes of presence as a wonderful circle. The Church is gathered and manifested in this local assembly (e.g., parish), and Christ is present. He becomes more so as the priest or bishop enters. The presence of Christ is intensified as the Word is read and expounded, all of these modes of presence leading up to the deepest, the sacramental presence of Christ in his Body and Blood. Still, wonderful as this special presence of Christ is, it is not an end in itself; rather, the Lord said "Take and eat; take and drink," and this presence in his Body and Blood is to transform us into his Body the Church, so we might become

47

more what we were when we gathered, only more so. The wonderful circle has been made, and we come back to where we began, only transformed more deeply.

28. What does "Real Presence" mean, and is this true of all the modes of Christ's presence in the Eucharist?

As the *Catechism* points out, Christ's presence in the Eucharist is *unique,* and it quotes Trent (D.S. 1651) to the effect that Christ is present "Body and Blood, together with the soul and divinity...and therefore the whole Christ is truly, really and substantially contained" (CCC no. 1374). This presence is called "real," not to say that the other modes of presence are not real, but to imply the greatest fullness of reality in this sacrament, that is to say, a *substantial* presence. "Real Presence" developed as a special term to distinguish it from a merely symbolic presence, said to be espoused by Berengar in the ninth century and by Zwinglians at the time of the Reformation. The Church, in using this term, wanted to safeguard the Eucharist from becoming seen as *only* a symbol or sign, though clearly the symbolism of bread and wine as signs of spiritual food and drink is part of the sacramental symbolism. We call this a special "sacramental presence," but unlike the other sacraments in which Christ is present in power while the sacrament is being celebrated, in the Blessed Sacrament he *remains* substantially as long as the elements remain. Because of this remaining "Real Presence," we can reserve the Eucharist for the sick, for those who need Communion outside of Mass times, and for prayer before the tabernacle.

The theology of the Eucharist enunciated by Vatican II tended to situate this presence of Christ in the celebration of the mysteries, as was the emphasis in the early Church, the personal presence of Christ in the holy meal, as has been previously explained. In the celebration of the great deed God has done in the saving death and resurrection of Christ now memorialized and made present through the prayer of praise and blessing called *berakah,* the Lord was experienced as dynamically present: what later generations would call "real."

29. Is this Catholic doctrine on the Real Presence one that goes back to the beginnings of the Church, or is it a medieval development?

Although some of the terminology we are used to using in the West, *substance* and *accident,* were theologically precised by the medieval doctors, most notably St. Thomas Aquinas (d. 1274), nonetheless the earliest apostolic fathers taught essentially the same teaching. St. Ignatius of Antioch (d. 107), said to be a disciple of St. Polycarp, a disciple of St. John the Evangelist, said, "…the bread is the flesh of Jesus, the Cup his blood" (Letter to the Smyrnaeans 7:1). St. Justin Martyr (d. 165) said, "Not as common food and drink do we receive these [elements], but since Jesus Christ our Savior was made incarnate by the Word of God and had both flesh and blood…so too…the food which has been made into the Eucharist by the Eucharistic Prayer set down by Him [Words of Institution] and by the change of which our blood and flesh is nourished is both the flesh and the blood of that incarnated Jesus" (First Apology 66). Sts. Irenaeus, Clement of Alexandria, Hippolytus, Cyprian, Cyril of Jerusalem, Ambrose, and Augustine all follow suit: saints and doctors of both East and West. Let us give the last words to St. Augustine (d. 411) and his mentor Ambrose (d. 405). The latter said "Christ is in that sacrament because it is the Body of Christ" (The Mysteries, 9:58), and the former "that bread which you see on the altar…is the Body of Christ. That chalice…is the Blood of Christ (Sermons, 227).

30. But isn't it true that transubstantiation is simply an Aristotelian explanation of Christ's presence in the Eucharist suitable for the Middle Ages?

The fathers of the Church tried to find ways of expressing the extraordinary change that takes place in the Eucharist and coined terms such as *transelementation, transfiguration,* based upon the prefix *trans,* which implies a process of going from one thing to another *through* a change. The roots of the term *transubstantiation* grew out of the eucharistic controversy of the ninth-century monastery of Corbie in France. The abbot, Pachase, wrote a book on Christ's presence in the Eucharist, which was so realistic that it scarcely distinguished Christ's bodily presence while on earth in the flesh from the sacramental presence in the Eucharist. Another monk of his monastery, Ratram, wrote a rejoinder, and using certain very spiritual texts from St. Augustine (who wrote so much that it was always possible to find him supporting many positions) saw almost exclusively a spiritual presence perceived by faith. He influenced Berengar (1010–88), who later proposed the presence of Christ as symbolic and said he was only mirroring Augustine. It may be true that he had a richer sense of symbol and Christ's presence in the symbol than was commonly understood at the time, but his symbolist position was taken on by Lanfranc, Archbishop of Canterbury, who upheld the fathers in recognizing the true Body of Christ in the Eucharist.

The term *transubstantiation* was first used by Stephen of Bruge (AD 1140), and curiously that was before the full corpus of Aristotle was reintroduced into the West. This suggests that the terms *substance* and *accidents* were first used as terms in attempting to explain a mystery of faith and not simply as reiterations of Aristotelian philosophy, although it is true that later St. Thomas Aquinas will probe the meaning of these terms to elucidate the eucharistic mystery. Transubstantiation was formally defined by the Church in 1215 at Lateran Council IV, the same council which insisted that Catholics receive Communion at least once a year at Eastertide. The Council of Trent was reacting to the Reformers' new teaching of Christ's presence as only a symbol, as Zwingli taught, or as simply a spiritual pledge of salvation, as Calvin taught. Luther held for a "Real Presence," but one that was not lasting because he held for consubstantiation, whereby the bread receives Christ as a poker receives heat, without any substantial

change. The Church taught in the Council of Trent: "By the consecration of the bread and wine, there takes place a change of the
whole substance of the bread into the substance of the Body of
our Lord and of the whole substance of the wine into the substance of his Blood. This change the Holy Catholic Church has
fittingly and properly called transubstantiation" (D.S. 1641 in
CCC no. 1376).

31. What do the terms *substance* and *accident* mean?

The Church teaches that the substance of the bread changes,
and that means the deepest reality of the bread changes and
becomes the Body of Christ, even though the accidents or appearances are the same color, texture, taste, etcetera. Substance philo-
sophically is being in itself, whereas appearances can only be in
something: one never simply sees a "red." Transubstantiation is
the clearest way that human reason has come up with to explain
how this substantial change on the deepest level of being can take
place when the external accidents of this reality remain the same.

We see accidental change when we see how the infant
changes to the child, to the adolescent, to the adult, to the elder,
and the person is the same even though the body undergoes many
changes. We see substantial and accidental change when we eat
some food and that food, for instance an apple, changes into our
being, losing both its substance and accidents. In this substantial
change the accidents of both bread and wine remain the same, but
on the deepest level of the being of these elements there is a
change so that the substance of bread and wine no longer remain,
but only Jesus: body and blood, soul and divinity, according to the
teaching of the Church.

32. Is Christ present in the Eucharist exactly as he was on earth?

St. Thomas masterfully treats this question in the third part
of the *Summa Theologiae* in Question 76. He sees the whole
Christ in the species of bread and wine, but not in a place as if

here and not there, that is, in heaven. Rather, he is present "as in the manner of a substance," so that when the host is consecrated he comes to be in this bread and wine on this altar, but not as if he were no longer in heaven. By the same token, he is substantially in the whole host so that breaking the host would not break his arm, because he is not present in a merely physical way, but more like that of a glorified body, which according to St. Thomas, has qualities beyond the physical, without forsaking its bodiliness (cf. S.T. Suppl qq 82–85). We are speaking of the physical in a way that goes beyond the physical—that is, the metaphysical—and this is what is meant by the substantial change. Perhaps a Jewish approach would be helpful here. The Jews saw the human person as enfleshed spirit: the person concretized in the body. So the Lord is present in his risen glorified body permeating the host with his presence. He is dynamically present there for us as a person as well as in heaven.

Christ remains present in the eucharistic species until the species (accidents) corrupts. If the consecrated bread is corrupted, then it no longer has the accidents or appearances of bread, and in such a case the Eucharistic Presence ceases to be there.

33. Shouldn't we use more contemporary terminology to describe this Eucharistic Presence?

Pope Paul VI raised the same question in *Mysterium Fidei* in the light of new theories of Christ's presence in the Eucharist: *transignification* and *transfinalization*. Transignification puts more emphasis on the *sign value* of the Eucharist so that the elements of bread and wine have new meaning, and transfinalization puts more emphasis on the finality or *purpose* of its elements. Still, we must know ultimately: what is it?—or should we say, who is it? It is true that our relationship with the Lord is the *purpose* of the Eucharist and that the bread and wine are *signs signifying* that purpose, but they can't do that if they are *only* signs, if the "what" of these signs is only bread and wine and not the Lord!

Pope Paul emphasized this very clearly but also pointed out that precision in terminology is essential lest misunderstandings of truth rise up. To this end he defended the use of dogmatic formulae that have risen in the Church's history and have been "canonized" by definitions of councils, for example, the use of the terms of *nature* and *person* used by the early trinitarian and christological councils and the eucharistic terminology of Lateran IV and Trent (cf. no. 24). He saw these terms as well adapted for all times and places. The pope did not forbid new approaches, but they must be in continuity with what the Church has always taught. One could not give the impression that eucharistic doctrine consisted "*only*" in transignification or transfinalization" without treating fully of transubstantiation (no. 11). John Paul II quoted Paul VI in *Ecclesia de Eucharistia* (no. 15) on this very point: "Every theological explanation which seeks some understanding of this mystery, in order to be in accord with Catholic faith, must firmly maintain that in objective reality, independently of our mind, the bread and wine have ceased to exist after the consecration, so that the adorable Body and Blood of the Lord Jesus from that moment on are really before us under the sacramental species of bread and wine."

34. How do we differ from our Protestant brethren on this point of Christ's presence in the Eucharist?

Classically, most Protestants followed Zwingli's dictum that Christ was present as "only in a memorial," not with the rich understanding that recent liturgical research has yielded as to the Jewish understanding of memorial (which we have seen), but with an understanding that equates it with a psychological memory alone. Most Protestants followed this view, but Luther's was not so radical. He always held for "Real Presence," but not in a way that the Church could accept. Luther held for Christ's presence in the eucharistic elements at the Consecration and at Communion by means of consubstantiation: that the Body and

Blood of Christ enter the elements as heat enters a poker thrust in the fire, but does not remain after. This the Church rejected because tradition holds for a lasting change of the elements as we have seen; still, had most Protestants followed this rather than Zwingli, Catholics and Protestants would be closer today. Zwingli held the Eucharist was "only a memorial," a remembrance of Christ with a spiritual significance, and most Protestant traditions followed this lead, but with the ecumenical sharing of theology and the deeper understanding of Jewish roots, many mainline churches are more open to a more Catholic approach, while among more Evangelical or Fundamentalist groups this is usually not the case.

35. What do the Orthodox believe on this point?

In general, Orthodox churches rest on Patristic formulations of the faith and do not like medieval Western Scholastic formulations (of Aquinas and the other doctors of the Schools [universities], hence the term *Scholastic*). This tends to be true of the Eucharist as well, although the seventeenth-century Ukrainian Orthodox theologian Peter Mogila formulated a catechism for the Orthodox Church in Ukraine-Russia, and the term "transubstantiation" is used in this book with the approval of the official Russian Church. They believe as we do on most questions, but they find Western terminology too confining. They prefer not to restrict the mystery, but perhaps lose precision in the process.

In the medieval West, there grew up a great devotion to the Blessed Sacrament reserved on, over, or near the altar. Hence, the ceremony of exposition and benediction developed, and the feast of Corpus Christi was instituted, but none of this development took place in the East. Eastern Christians believe that Christ dwells in the church building and would not deny that it was true of the elements reserved on the altar, but their attention would more likely be drawn to the icons on the Iconostasis (icon stand or screen) than the Eucharistic Presence, which they are more likely to recognize in the

Divine Liturgy itself. Catholic groups that are united to Rome have been influenced by that fact, and many have some form of exposition according to their liturgical tradition.

36. Is it the Words of Institution or the *Epiclesis* that consecrates the elements in the Eucharist?

We have seen how there are two *Epicleses* in most of the Eucharistic Prayers used by the Church; one is a prayer for the Holy Spirit to consecrate the elements of bread and wine or to transform them into the Body and Blood of Christ; the other is a prayer to the Spirit that those who receive the Body and Blood of the Lord might be one Body in Christ, and is therefore a prayer for the unity of the Church. The earliest *Epiclesis* seems to be the latter form, and we find this in the ancient Eucharistic Prayer of the *Didache* (AD 110): "Just as this broken bread was scattered on the hillside [as grain] and made one, so may your Church be gathered into one" (no. 9). The East began to explicate the action of the Spirit in changing the elements (all works of sanctification are attributed to the Spirit), and in many Eucharistic Prayers this *Epiclesis* came after the Words of Institution (e.g., St. Basil, St. John Chrysostom).

The tradition of the West developed in focusing on Christ's Word and so saw the action of the Spirit in the Words of Institution, as we have seen in the quotation from St. Justin Martyr (cf. no. 28). St. Ambrose echoes this and sees the Word (Christ) acting through the words (De Sac. IV 4.14–17). The celebrant holds the eucharistic elements up for adoration, which would make no sense if we did not believe each element had been changed into the Body of the Lord and shortly thereafter, his Blood. The adage *lex orandi lex credendi* implies that this development, this articulation of the faith, is legitimate and valid.

The East and West articulated the mysteries differently, and as they grew more separated from each other (after 1054), positions began to harden, with the East saying it was *only* through the

Epiclesis that the elements were changed while the West held *only* to the Words. In a more ecumenical era, with the practices of each tradition more thoroughly studied, there seems to be less of an obstacle toward rapprochement over this issue than perhaps there was before. The new Eucharistic Prayers of the Roman Rite all have two *Epicleses,* as has been explained above, although this is not true of the Roman Canon, which may have an *Epiclesis* in other words. All, both East and West, admit that this marvelous change is the work of the Spirit empowering the Words of Institution as well as the *Epiclesis.* Finally the East of course says the Words of Institution to memorialize what Jesus did and admits that their presence is necessary, while all in East and West tend to focus more on the totality of the Eucharistic Prayer rather than on its parts. Eastern Catholics, after all, have used the prayers of Sts. Basil and John Chrysostom, and Rome has always accepted the validity of these formularies.

Recently, the Church recognized the Eucharist celebrated by the Assyrian Church of the East, which uses the ancient Eucharistic Prayer of Addai and Mari, one that has no Words of Institution and seems not to have had them from time immemorial. The document, dated October 26, 2001, and signed by Pope John Paul II, allows Chaldean Catholics to receive Communion in Assyrian churches when they are deprived of a priest of their own church. The Church recognizes the validity of Assyrian orders, but the surprising element is Rome's recognition of the validity of the Canon of Addai and Mari, which has no Words of Institution.

A statement from the Vatican Council for Christian Unity pointed out that the Church sees the Words of Institution as a constitutive part of the Eucharistic Prayer. How then can the Church accept a Canon without these words? The Church does not have power over the substance of the sacraments, but she has the power to determine their signs and formularies. This ancient prayer (like the *Didache*) never seemed to have the words, but the intention of the Assyrian Church was always to consecrate the elements so that they became the Body and Blood of Christ. Their other

Canons do have the Words of Institution. The document states that the Canon of Addai and Mari have these words not explicitly but implicitly "in a dispersed way from the beginning to the end, in the most important passages of the Anaphora" (Eucharistic Prayer). So the Holy Spirit can work through the words spread throughout this Eucharistic Prayer.

Six

Communing with Christ in the Eucharist

37. What are the conditions for a worthy communion?

The whole point of this sacrament is that we "Take...and eat....Take and drink." However, St. Paul tells us that "all who eat and drink without discerning the body, eat and drink judgment against themselves" (1 Cor 11:29), and the Church interprets this as discerning that one is free of serious or mortal sin. Mortal or deadly sin (cf. 1 John 5:16) kills the life of God or grace in the soul and sets a person in opposition to God, and such a person does not have the right disposition to receive the Lord. The sacrament of penance or reconciliation is called for, not every time before Communion, but only when one is conscious of grave sin in one's life or on one's conscience. Venial sins, or light sins, are forgiven by this sacrament of the Eucharist, as the fathers and St. Thomas teach, and this is echoed by the *Catechism* (cf. CCC no. 1394) because this is the sacrament of the Blood of Jesus, "shed for many for the forgiveness of sins." Even if one is not conscious of mortal sin, sacramental confession of venial sins regularly is recommended by the Church (CCC no. 1458) as a way of "keeping fit," of forming our conscience, of healing, of growth in the Spirit.

One must also fast for one hour from solid food and liquids other than water (cf. CIC, can. 919), although illness can reduce this fast to a quarter of an hour, or for very serious illness none at all (cf. *Eucharistiae Sacramentum,* no. 24). The hour required is time before Communion and not before the beginning of the Mass. If one were lacking a few minutes, many moral theologians would call that a "moral hour" and would say it was licit to receive in such a situation.

The Church obliges us to come to Mass on Sundays and holy days of obligation but does not command Communion, although she highly encourages it, since it is communion with the "flesh of the risen Christ...giving life through the Holy

Spirit...[it] preserves, increases, and renews the life of grace received at Baptism." (CCC no. 1392). Because of this great sacrament's deepest reality, when receiving the Body and Blood of the Lord, we must prepare ourselves as we have described above. Finally, we should be suitably clothed and respectful in posture to show the "solemnity and joy of this moment when Christ becomes our guest" (cf. CCC no. 1387).

The Code of Canon Law obliges all Catholics to receive the Eucharist at least once a year, if possible, during the Easter season (canon 920). The canon specifies that one should be prepared by the sacrament of reconciliation, although most canonists would say that if one were not conscious of mortal sin, one need not confess. It seems to me though, that now the problem is not that people are not staying away from Communion because of feelings of unworthiness, but rather that everyone goes and very few seem to utilize the sacrament of penance or reconciliation. For all of us, ongoing conversion would bring us to confession even for light sins, to grow and be healed, a process that the Eucharist facilitates. Yearly confession and Communion comprise the barest minimum of Catholic life.

38. How do I know if I'm in a state of mortal or serious sin?

The *Catechism* summarizes the Catholic tradition in defining mortal sin as "sin whose object is grave matter which is also committed with full knowledge and deliberate consent" (CCC no. 1857). This means that what one has done must be of its nature a serious matter in itself. The only way stealing a quarter would be serious was if it were molded into a bullet to kill the pope! This would mean, of course, that another intention had given this venial act a far more serious orientation. Sexual matter is always serious because one is dealing with the power to pass on life in sexual intercourse, but not all sexual sins are mortal. All three conditions must be present for serious sin.

Besides grave matter, there must be full knowledge that this act is a mortal sin. Often in our somewhat confused state of knowledge about the Catholic faith, people may quite sincerely be in ignorance that certain practices are sinful, even seriously so — one could think of masturbation, premarital sex, business fraud, cheating, and so forth. However, if one begins to wonder, then one has an obligation to find the truth of the matter. Ignorance may excuse, but not after one's conscience has been informed, and we do have an obligation to so inform ourselves.

Finally, there must be deliberate consent. If my freedom is taken away by force, for instance, rape, psychological brainwashing or manipulation, or by addiction, then I am not culpable for the act as a mortal sin, although in the case of addiction I may be responsible for its beginning.

Sin that is grave is not easy to fall into. It takes some doing, but if one finds oneself in such a state, one should get to the tribunal of mercy and reconciliation as quickly as possible to be reinstated in one's friendship with the Lord. Also, the sacrament of reconciliation is a great help in fighting a habit of serious sin when honestly used with regularity. Yearly confession along with one's Easter Duty of Communion keeps one in communion with the Lord and his Church, but that is a bare minimum. Frequent confession and Communion keep one in loving, vital communion with the Lord and his Church, which is to be desired. Finally, *Redemptionis Sacramentum* underlines the fact that those conscious of being in the state of grave sin ought to confess before receiving the Eucharist (no. 81).

39. Does a priest in serious sin still celebrate a valid Mass?

Yes, he does, because God is more concerned with the good of the people at Mass, who would be deprived of the Eucharist if the serious sins of the clergy canceled out the validity of the sacraments. This question first arose in the early fourth century when the followers of Donatus (hence called Donatists) refused to accept the ministry of a bishop of Carthage in AD 311 who had been a traitor to the faith during savage persecution. He had repented, but they would not accept him, nor any clergy whom they judged to be sinful—how can a sinner pass on grace? St. Augustine (d. 430) waged war against this error by pointing out that Christ worked through the priestly character *(sacramentum manens)* of the sacrament of holy orders, even if the priest himself were not in a state of grace. He was an instrument of the sinless Christ who would work through him for the sake of the people. This remains the clear teaching of the Church to this day, so that even if a priest is personally sinful, Christ works through him and brings me the sacrament, which I can receive from him.

If a priest were to be in this unhappy state and if it were necessary for him to celebrate Mass without the opportunity for confession, he should make a perfect act of contrition, celebrate Mass for the sake of the people, and get to confession as soon as possible. This principle would also apply to layfolk if they are in a similar situation and have *grave reason* for receiving Holy Communion with *no possibility* for confession. This is spelled out in canon 916 of the Code of Canon Law, but only in very grave situations, because the Church clearly teaches, echoing Trent, that all mortal sins must be confessed by species (type of sin) and number (approximate) before receiving Communion (cf. CCC nos. 1456, 1457). Accordingly, those who use this provision of the law are to mention their sins at their next confession.

40. How can I receive Communion? On the tongue? In the hand?

Before Vatican Council II, the standard way that Roman Catholics received Communion was kneeling at an altar rail and as they opened their mouths and stuck out their tongues, the priest put the host directly on the tongue. This was basically the way that medieval Catholics received Communion. Pope Paul VI in *Memoriale Domini* (1969) allowed the ancient practice of receiving

Communion in the hand if the bishops' conference of a given region asked for that permission. Then the right hand was to be held over the left and "an altar or throne" was to be made of the hands so that the other hand could take the host and lift it to the mouth to be swallowed. Also permission was given to stand, as our forebears in the faith in the early Church did, as a sign of the resurrection, whereas kneeling was often seen as penitential in the early Church. The American bishops have mandated standing (although bishops may make exceptions), though not all bishops have mandated it. When standing is the normal way to receive, a reverence is to be made beforehand. Our bishops have mandated a common reverence before Communion in the bowing of one's head as the person before one receives. This common gesture, which gives unity to our liturgical celebrations, ought to be followed, though some tolerance for various ethnic or regional pious customs is also required.

41. Is the celebrant of the Mass or the minister of Communion the arbiter of how I receive Communion?

It is up to me whether I receive on the tongue as my medieval forbears in the faith did, or in the hand as my early Christian forebears did. In this case father does not know best.

As to kneeling for Communion, since the bishops of our country have opted for standing, we ought to follow that practice unless we're attending an authorized preconciliar Mass or are in a parish to which the local bishop has granted an exception. When I bow before Communion, it ought to be done while the person before me receives so I can be ready for my turn. Though kneeling is discouraged, should a person kneel, he ought not to be refused Communion (R.S. no. 91).

42. Why do all stand for the Eucharistic Prayer in some churches and in others, all kneel?

The General Instruction of the Roman Missal (GIRM) of 1969 directed that the congregation stand from the Prayer over the

Gifts until the end of Mass and that they should kneel for the Consecration (no. 21). This is widely followed in northern Europe. However, the same legislation allows conferences of bishops to adapt the postures and gestures to accord with the sensibilities of our own people. Accordingly the American bishops, being aware of the Irish tradition of kneeling for Mass (in Ireland today, they kneel much more for Mass than we do), petitioned the Holy See for a rescript to kneel from after the *Sanctus* or "Holy, holy" until after the Great Amen at the end of the Eucharistic Prayer. A rescript is an exception to the law that becomes a law itself, and so the Church in America has this liturgical custom. At times this custom has been questioned by liturgists wanting to conform to the more ancient custom of standing during the Canon, as was done by the early Church, but our bishops, I think, wisely have stuck by their pastoral decision. The new General Instruction (2001) lauds kneeling at this time where it is the custom (no. 43). The law does provide for not kneeling for the Consecration where there is a lack of space, density of the crowd, or other reasonable cause (ibid.). One thinks of crowded papal Masses at St. Peter's or World Youth Day Masses and similar Masses in stadia, parks, or arenas of large cities. Standing has always been seen as a sign of the resurrection by the Eastern Church and by the early Church in the West, whereas kneeling was seen as more penitential. In matters where there are various traditions in liturgical matters, we should be guided by our bishops.

43. How come some parishes offer the chalice and others do not?

Vatican Council II restored the chalice as an option after perhaps a thousand-year hiatus. Drinking from the cup as well as receiving the consecrated bread was the way the early Christians received Communion, but as people received less and less frequently and as medieval precision developed in eucharistic theology that the Lord was in his Body and Blood concomitantly under both signs, there seemed to be no need for the cup. John Hus and the Utraquists (from *utraque* or "both," for "both species") wanted Communion restored under *both* species or forms: bread and wine. Martin Luther took up the same cry, but now it was joined to other propositions the Church considered erroneous, so this possible reform became associated with heresy and was therefore ignored.

One might note the Eastern Christians, both Catholic and Orthodox, have *always* received under both species. The bread that is consecrated is leavened, cut up into small cubes, and placed in the chalice filled with the consecrated wine. The communicant comes forward, holds his head back, opens his or her mouth with tongue back in the mouth, and the celebrant, using a little golden spoon that holds the Body of the Lord soaked in the Precious Blood, deposits it in the communicant's mouth without the spoon touching the mouth. This is called intinction in the West and may be done with the minister dipping the host into the Precious Blood in the chalice and placing both species directly on the tongue (and not in the hand, for obvious reasons).

Liturgists, aware of this practice as well as the ancient practice of the early Church, were asking for the restoration of the chalice to the laity at the time of Vatican Council II. Hence the Constitution on the Sacred Liturgy allowed the practice according to the judgment of the bishop, and three examples were given: the newly baptized, newly professed, and the newly ordained (no. 55). As new documentation emerged after the council, this list kept expanding, adding more occasions for using this permission (e.g., *Eucharisticum Mysterium* no. 32) until the document *This Holy and Living Sacrifice,* issued by the American Bishops in 1985 and approved by the Vatican, states that Communion may be given under both species at any time as long as the numbers are not so great as to preclude the proper reverence (no. 22). The General Instruction of the Roman Missal makes it clear that Trent teaches that Christ is received whole and entire in a complete sacrament even when people receive under one kind only; still it encourages Communion under both forms:

Holy Communion has a more complete form as a sign when it is received under both kinds. For in this manner of reception, a fuller sign of the Eucharistic banquet shines forth. Moreover, there is a clearer expression of that will by which the new and everlasting covenant is ratified in the Blood of the Lord and of that relationship of the Eucharistic banquet to the eschatological banquet in the Father's Kingdom. (no. 281)

44. Why is it that there are different traditions as to when one might receive one's First Communion?

In the early Church, when there were many adult converts to the faith, one became a Christian by being baptized, confirmed, and receiving the Eucharist all at once, usually during the Easter Vigil. As there were fewer adults in some cultures to convert, the demand for infant baptism began to be heard. This practice seems always to have existed, for we read in the New Testament of whole households being baptized (cf. Acts 16:33; 1 Cor 1:16), and Hippolytus in the *Apostolic Tradition* states: "...for those who can't answer for themselves [children] let another do so...," (no. 21) speaking of the prebaptismal interrogation. Consequently, as infant baptisms more and more became the practice of the Church, it changed the interrelatedness of the three sacraments of Christian initiation in different ways: one for the East and one for the West.

In the Christian East the three sacraments remained together, performed by the priest, who first baptized infants, then confirmed or "chrismated" them, as the East would say, and then gave them Holy Communion. This practice perdures among many of the Orthodox to this day, and among some Eastern Catholics as well. A recent document from the Holy See encourages those Eastern Churches that had "First Communion" at seven years of age like the West to return to their more pristine practice. A practice similar to this is found among Hispanics, particularly among Mexicans.

In the West, priests baptized infants, but the completion of confirmation was reserved to the bishop when he was able to get around, and one's First Communion took place around that time, so that the order of the sacraments of Christian initiation was largely intact. The age at which confirmation and First Communion took place varied from the age of reason through adolescence, but the latter age was more common. Pope St. Pius X, in *Quam Singulari* (1910), changed the practice by lowering the age for First Communion universally to the age of reason, commonly computed to be seven years of age. This changed the usual order for the sacraments of Christian initiation as seen above to that of baptism, Eucharist, and confirmation. Many liturgists today, not liking this change, propose that we communicate infants (unlikely to happen) or prepare children for first confession, First Communion, and confirmation at roughly the same time to bring these sacraments into closer proximity, perhaps liturgically desirable, but catechetically a tall order. As it stands now, the age for the sacrament of confirmation in the United States ranges from seven to sixteen.

45. How often may I receive Holy Communion?

In the early Church, although the Eucharist was celebrated only on Sundays, still daily Communion was often practiced, with the father of the family bringing home the consecrated Eucharist in a pyx for the family to receive during the week. Tertullian (d. 225) was recorded as instructing Christians to be sure the pyx (box) was secure so that mice might not get into it. Curiously, as Mass was celebrated more frequently by monk priests, even daily in medieval times, fewer and fewer Christians went to Communion. Various reasons are alleged: The conversion of the northern barbarians coupled with a heavy anti-Arian polemic that possibly overemphasized Christ's divinity may have left many of the newly converted with the idea that the Eucharist could only be rarely received, for who could be worthy to receive his God as food? Ironically, the very council that defined transubstantiation (IV Lateran in 1215) had to insist that Catholic Christians receive

Communion *at least once a year* during the Easter season. This was called the Easter Duty.

Catholics in the Counter-Reformation period rarely received Communion and that is why various confraternities and sodalities pushed monthly Communion. Religious were only allowed to receive on certain days. Is that why the Lord as the Sacred Heart in his apparitions to St. Margaret Mary Alacoque (1673–75) had her propagate Communion in reparation on the nine First Fridays to combat the Jansenistic (Puritanical) influence in France? Many may remember the Holy Name Sundays when the men of the parish went to Communion in a body and then had a Communion breakfast after. And the Mother's Club and the Rosary Altar Society would follow suit, with a group Communion and breakfast afterward.

Pope St. Pius X restored frequent or even daily Communion to all Catholics, provided they were free of serious sin and had kept the Communion fast, which in his day consisted of not eating any food from midnight and no liquid except water for the same time. Consequently one may now receive Communion daily. The instruction *Immensae Caritatis* of 1973 expanded the times when one could receive again, and now the Code of Canon Law permits reception of Communion "for a second time if for legitimate reasons one were attending another Mass on the same day" (no. 917). Communion is the normal way to fully participate at Mass, and if one had a liturgical ministry at another Mass or if one were there on a special occasion, one could receive again. Clearly the intention of the law is not to go to as many Masses as possible on a given day so as to receive as many times as possible.

46. What is the Communion fast?

When the Eucharist was celebrated in the Roman Empire in the very early morning, the tradition was that receiving the Eucharist broke one's fast before breakfast. This custom remained the custom until Pius XII permitted afternoon and evening Masses in 1953. He accordingly reduced the fasting from food and all liquids except water to three hours before Communion. *Immensae Caritatis* of 1973 reduced this fast from food and liquids other than water to one hour before Communion and further allowed it to be only fifteen minutes for the ill and the elderly, or not even that if serious conditions warranted not fasting at all. The present Code of Canon Law (canon 919) requires a fast from food and liquids for an hour before Communion (water and medicine do not break the fast) and no fast at all for the old and the ill or for those who are actually caring for them.

47. What are the fruits of Holy Communion?

St. Thomas in the *Summa Theologiae* sees these fruits as a fullness of grace bestowed from Christ, venial sins forgiven, temporal punishment due to sin (in purgatory) remitted, and preservation from sin in the future (S.T. III q 80). The *Catechism of the Catholic Church* (nos. 1391–93) sees Communion as augmenting "intimate union with Christ Jesus," for he said, "Those who eat my flesh and drink my blood abide in me and I in them" (John 6:56). He it is who gives us life in the Holy Spirit by this sacrament that preserves, increases, and renews the life of grace received at baptism. It cleanses us from past sins and preserves us from future sins and restores lost strength so that charity is strengthened. "This living charity wipes away venial sins..." (Trent quoted in CCC no. 1394). It makes us more the Church: We, "though many, are one body..." (1 Cor 12:12), and commits us to the poor (CCC no. 1397). We see many of the same emphases of St. Thomas, perhaps more fulsomely spelled out, and this does not surprise us for it is the same Lord and the same Eucharist celebrated for the same Church.

John Paul II in *Ecclesia de Eucharistia* echoed this teaching, and he further emphasized growth in the Holy Spirit through the Eucharist, quoting St. Ephrem: "He called the bread his living Body and he filled it with himself and His Spirit.…He who eats it with faith, eats Fire and Spirit" (no. 17). He also emphasized the Eucharist as building the communion of the Church (ch. 2).

48. Can those who are invalidly married receive Communion?

Since such a couple would not be married in the eyes of God or the Church, they may not receive Communion unless they are able to live as brother and sister. In *Familiaris Consortio,* John Paul II notes that sometimes after the breakup of a valid marriage, people enter a second union for the sake of the children. Sometimes they are convinced that their previous marriage had never been valid, even though they could not have it annulled. The pope reaffirmed the practice of not admitting divorced and remarried people to Communion without an annulment, although the Church still shows motherly care for them and for their children (nos. 28, 29).

49. What is a Spiritual Communion?

This is a pious practice based on the teaching of the medieval doctors that one may receive the grace of the sacrament even if one can't receive the form. For example, when one can't get to confession, one tries to make a perfect act of contrition so as to be reconciled with God from the motive of being sorry for having offended him and not simply from a servile fear of hell. So also a "Spiritual Communion" is recommended for those who couldn't fast or are from another church or are in a bad marriage, that although they cannot partake of the sacred banquet, they commune with Christ by prayer and pray that he will visit them by grace if not sacramentally. The theology behind this practice is that with perfect contrition and a desire to be in unity with the Church, some aspects of the reality of the sacrament can come to the person even if one is unable to receive the sacrament itself, the Body and Blood of Christ.

50. Are there healing aspects of the Eucharist?

The *Catechism* states that "what material food produces in our bodily life, Holy Communion wonderfully achieves in our spiritual life" (no. 1392). Since it is the risen Lord we receive who gives us the life-giving Spirit, we are not surprised that the Spirit preserves, increases, and renews baptismal grace (ibid.). Only penance (the sacrament) can forgive mortal sin, but the Eucharist can forgive venial sin, as we have seen. In a sense, the Eucharist is a healing sacrament in preventing sin, causing life to flourish, and in dealing with the effects of sin. One priest-counselor who had many clients installed an oratory near his office where his clients prayed before the Blessed Sacrament exposed in the monstrance. He told them to gaze on the sacrament encased in the sunburst monstrance (a very common motif) and to imagine the rays of grace energizing them from the Body of the risen Lord. They felt less need to talk to him, less need for his help and counsel. One young woman who led an unconverted life told me that after her conversion she loved to gaze on the Blessed Sacrament to cleanse her eyes from things she ought not to have seen. There are many ways the Eucharist heals. St. Teresa of Avila said in her *Way of Perfection:*

> And do not imagine that this most sacred food is not an excellent food for our bodies and a splendid remedy even for bodily ills! I know for a fact that it is. I know a person [meaning herself] who suffered from serious illness and was often in the greatest pain, that that pain was lifted from her when she received the Eucharist so that she felt completely well.

51. Are the healings from the Eucharist physical, psychological, or spiritual?

St. Paul speaks of us as being made of spirit, soul, and body (1 Thess 5:23). Our psychological life (*psyche* in Greek means "soul") interacts with our spiritual life since our spirit is the deepest part of us—the soul of our soul—where we can be touched by the Holy Spirit. Finally, we are not just spirits or angels but enfleshed spirits with bodies that influence our inner life. I once met a woman at Lourdes who worked at the Medical Bureau there. She had been brought to Lourdes paralyzed on a pallet. As she was blessed with the Eucharist in the Blessed Sacrament procession, she could feel movement in her limbs, but also as she experienced the Eucharist and the great love that the Lord had for her, she felt the paralysis of her bitterness disappearing. She was healed physically, psychologically, and spiritually. All of these aspects of us interact with one another, as medical science is recognizing more and more. My novice master had a disease of the throat, and as he drank the Precious Blood at Mass he prayed that he would be healed — and he was.

St. Augustine in his *Retractions* states that he didn't credit sufficiently the healings that occurred in the celebration of the Eucharist. St. Paul states that unworthy reception of the Eucharist, that is, in sin, was the reason many were not healed in the Corinthian community (1 Cor 11:30).

52. What are the Roman guidelines for healing Masses?

An Instruction of the Congregation for the Doctrine of the Faith (Nov. 23, 2000) cautioned against sensationalism in Masses for healing. The emphasis is to be on the Lord, who is present in the Eucharist as a healer, not on the priest-celebrant regardless of what his healing gifts may be. Perhaps some priests with a healing charism have drawn too much attention to themselves, which would be wrong since the charisms are for the sake of the Church and not oneself (cf. CCC no. 799). The document also cautions against anything that would work the assembly up, but emphasizes the need for peace. The document emphasizes as well that the proper rubrics of the liturgy and approved liturgical formularies and Masses be followed. The Church here is concerned not to stifle the charism of healing but to be concerned that all things be done decently and in order (cf. CCC no. 801).

In nonliturgical prayers for healing, there is greater freedom, but a warning against hysteria, artificiality, theatricality, or sensationalism is sounded, as well as against blurring the distinction between the liturgical and the nonliturgical. Finally, exorcisms are forbidden at healing services, whether liturgical or nonliturgical.

53. Can Orthodox Christians receive at our Mass?

When the question of intercommunion arises, it is very important to realize that the Eucharist is at the very center of the unity of the Church. Eating the Body of the Lord makes one more completely a member of the Body of the Church, as we have pointed out. It is clear that Catholics in good standing may receive Communion in any rite of the Catholic Church, the more numerous churches of the Western or Roman Rite, or in any of the various Eastern Catholic rites. The Orthodox churches and other Eastern churches not united to Rome still have valid orders in their priesthood; their priests are truly priests, and they have the sacrament of the Eucharist, which they receive. Because they are so close to us in belief and with ecclesial permission of their hierarchy, on certain occasions they may receive at the Catholic Eucharist (cf. CCC no. 1399). This was reiterated by John Paul II in *Ecclesia de Eucharistia,* where he stated that the Eucharist may be given to "Eastern Christians separated in good faith from the Catholic Church, who spontaneously ask to receive the Eucharist from a Catholic minister" (no. 45). As regards the Eastern churches, the *Catechism* quotes the Decree on Ecumenism, *Unitatis Redintegratio,* that "such sharing given suitable circumstances and the approval of Church authority, is not merely possible but is encouraged" (U.R. 15 § 2 in CCC no. 1399).

54. Can Protestants receive Communion at Catholic Mass?

As we stated before, Communion in the Body of the Lord makes us one in Christ, but this unfortunately is not true of those

Christians who have totally different doctrines regarding Christ's presence in the Eucharist. Officially Protestants are called ecclesial communities because they do not have valid orders. In effect if we allowed wide intercommunion we'd be saying that we are all one doctrinally, organically, and ecclesially, but that simply is not true, and yet we rejoice in what we do share together: a common baptism in Christ and a love of his Word. In general then, the Church does not allow Protestants to receive Catholic Communion. However, if there is a grave necessity and the bishop concurs, the sacraments may be given to those Christians who hold the Catholic understanding of the sacraments, who approach freely, and are rightly disposed (cf. CCC no. 1401). This is more likely to be the case for Anglicans, Episcopalians, Lutherans, and perhaps Methodists rather than those ecclesial bodies with a less sacramental tradition. *Ecclesia de Eucharistia* makes the point that while

> "...it is never legitimate to concelebrate in the absence of full communion, the same is not true with respect to the administration of the Eucharist under special circumstances, to individual[s]...[in] Ecclesial Communities not in full communion with the Catholic Church. In this case, in fact, the intention is to meet a grave spiritual need for the eternal salvation of an individual believer, not to bring about an intercommunion which remains impossible until the visible bonds of ecclesial communion are fully established." (no. 45)

So while in certain instances of grave necessity, Communion may be given to Protestants, *concelebration* of Catholic priests with those who do not have apostolic succession is a grave offense that must be referred to the Congregation for the Doctrine of the Faith in Rome (R.S. no. 172c) because concelebration of the clergy implies a eucharistic unity we do not yet share.

55. Can Jews or Muslims receive Communion at Catholic Mass?

It is clear that we are indebted to our Old Testament forebears in the faith whose belief in the Promise is carried on by their Jewish descendants. We who are the People of God in the New Covenant are linked with them, God's People of the Old Covenant (N.A. 4; cf. CCC no. 839). Therefore, any kind of anti-Semitism held on to by a Catholic Christian is reprehensible and offensive to the Lord Jesus, born to that race of his Jewish maiden mother. However, the Eucharist is an act of faith in Christ as Lord and Messiah, a faith our Jewish brothers and sisters cannot accept, so it would be dishonest for them to take Communion or for us to invite them.

Our Muslim brothers and sisters acknowledge God, see Jesus as a great prophet, and honor his mother (who appeared in 1917 at a little village, Fatima, named after Muhammad's daughter). But they too, like other non-Christians, do not believe that Jesus is the Son of God and that the Eucharist is his Body and Blood and our way to be nourished by him in this life, so likewise, it would be dishonest for us to invite them to receive or for them to do so.

Interfaith and ecumenical cooperation on issues of "justice and peace, support for family life, respect for minority communities" is highly recommended by the *Ecumenical Directory* (no. 210), and such cooperation and collaboration encourages mutual understanding.

56. On the other hand, can we receive at the Divine Liturgy (the Eucharist) celebrated by the Eastern Orthodox or by other Eastern Christians with valid orders?

We have seen that we may always receive in Eastern Catholic Rites and that there can be a certain intercommunion with Eastern non-Catholic churches whose orders we recognize as valid (cf. CCC no. 1399). Usually there has been some common agreement between the Catholic Church and the particular Eastern church. Some Orthodox churches (in the Middle East) are more open to this and others are not (Russia, Greece, Ukraine, etc.). To some degree one would have more reason to avail one-self of this opportunity if one were traveling and a Catholic church were not readily available. One would need the priest's permission, and the Orthodox are often stricter on this point than the Catholic Church. One may always fulfill one's Sunday obli-gation at their Divine Liturgy even if not communicating. We have seen John Paul II's teaching on intercommunion with Eastern Christians separated from Rome in *Ecclesia de Eucharistia* (no. 45), but in that same document, he pointed out that "in particular circumstances, Catholics too can request these same sacraments from ministers of Churches in which these sacraments are valid" (no. 46). He was speaking of the sacraments of Eucharist, penance, and anointing of the sick, which may be given in danger of death or when a Catholic priest is not available, but only "from a minister in whose Church these sacraments are valid or from one who is known to be validly ordained according to the Catholic teaching on ordination" (*Ecumenical Directory,* Council for Christian Unity: 1993, no. 132).

57. May one receive at an Anglican (Episcopalian) Eucharist?

This is a complex question because often the Anglican or Episcopal service seems very similar to ours and is often more like Mass used to be than our current rite. Even though their "High Church" party has always emphasized the Catholic dimensions of Anglicanism, there is also a "Low Church" or Evangelical party that emphasizes a more Protestant approach, and this was particu-larly true of Cranmer, the author of the Book of Common Prayer. While he had a great gift of translating prayers of the *Roman Missal* into exquisite English, he tended to be more Zwinglian in his approach to the Eucharist, changing the words to eliminate the concept of sacrifice, as well as transubstantiation. Because of this, when the question of the validity of Anglican orders was studied by the Vatican in response to the query of interested parties in

1896, *Apostolicae Curae* of Pope Leo XIII was issued, stating that for reasons just given Anglican orders were not valid in the Roman Catholic sense. Thus Anglican Eucharist is not the same as Catholic Mass or the Divine Liturgy celebrated by Eastern Catholics or Eastern Orthodox. Therefore Catholics may not receive at an Anglican Eucharist. It is true that many Anglicans consider themselves Catholic and that after *Apostolicae Curae,* some Anglican clergy got themselves ordained by churchmen with valid orders so that some Anglican Eucharists may be valid. Nonetheless, when Anglican clergy are accepted by Rome, they are always reordained. This shows that the Church does not see Anglicanism as fully Catholic and therefore not acceptable for intercommunion, although we must rejoice with them in the Catholic elements they do share and pray for a fuller unity with them in the future. Number 132 of the *Ecumenical Directory* of the Council for Christian Unity just quoted applies here: Catholics may receive "only from a minister in whose Church the sacraments are valid or from one who is known to be validly ordained according to the Catholic teaching on ordination."

58. Can we receive at a Protestant Eucharist?

Often some Lutheran or Methodist services of the Eucharist will seem similar to our Mass, and it is not surprising since their liturgical patrimony was that of the Catholic Church. However, they do not see the Eucharist as we do, even though Lutherans may hold for "Real Presence" as opposed to the Zwinglianism of most Protestants. Still they do not see their ministers as priests and so lost the understanding of priesthood and sacrifice as well as transubstantiation; thus intercommunion for us is an impossibility. We've seen however that the Jewish concept of "memorial" is opening many Protestant scholars to consider priesthood and sacrifice in a new way (as indeed Catholics are as well), and we pray that a deeper agreement be brought about by study, prayer, and sharing now those things we do have in common. *Ecclesia de Eucharistia* affirms the need for ecumenical dialogue for working toward greater Christian unity (no. 43), but also states clearly that since "...the Church's unity, which the Eucharist brings about through the Lord's sacrifice and by communion in his Body and Blood requires full communion in the bonds of the profession of faith, it is not possible to celebrate together the same Eucharistic liturgy until these bonds are re-established" (no. 44). Further, in the light of the above, he states: "Catholics may not receive communion in those communities which lack a valid sacrament of Orders" (no. 46).

59. Who are the ministers of Holy Communion? Who are the extraordinary ministers?

Bishops, priests, and deacons are the ordinary ministers of the Eucharist in terms of the distribution, whereas only bishops and priests celebrate the Eucharist. *Immensae Caritatis,* issued in 1973, allowed for extraordinary ministers of Holy Communion to help in the distribution of Communion. Not only can they be used when the ordinary ministers listed above (including instituted acolytes) cannot, but also when there are so many to communicate "that the celebration of the Mass would be unduly prolonged" (no. 1c), and when one considers the large crowds at Mass in the United States and especially when Communion is administered under both species, one can see why the American bishops have made use of this ministry to help the ordinary minister. They are not to be employed when there are ordinary ministers sitting in the sanctuary not fulfilling their function (R.S. no. 157). Extraordinary ministers are to be examples to the other faithful by their piety and reverence for this holy sacrament (cf. no. 6). Canon 910 makes it clear that the ordinary ministers are bishops, priests, and deacons, and extraordinary ministers, when needed, are the acolytes and others of the faithful who may be designated.

60. What is Viaticum and how is it administered?

Viaticum is the Eucharist received at the moment of "passing over," or death. The Eucharist is received so that Christ is with you, *"te cum,"* on the way, *"in via,"*—hence the name *Viaticum:* Christ to be with us on the way into eternal life. "Those who eat my flesh and drink my blood have eternal life, and I will raise them up on the last day" (John 6:54). These are the last rites that follow the anointing of the ill.

The ritual for Viaticum can be within Mass at the dying person's bedside, or Viaticum may be given without the celebration of Mass. In any event, a distinctive feature of the celebration is the renewal of the baptismal promises after the homily. It is the renewal and fulfillment of initiation into the Christian mysteries of Christ's death and resurrection and our "passing over" in our baptism and the Eucharist. A kiss of peace may be given as a leave-taking of the one dying with the hope of reunion in eternal life. For Viaticum, Communion may be given under both species. This is easily done at Mass, but if not, then the hosts are brought in a pyx and the Precious Blood is put in the tabernacle until the time when it is transported in a sealed vessel with no danger of spilling. After Viaticum, any of the Precious Blood that is left is consumed by the minister, and the vessel is properly purified. If the dying person lingers on, Viaticum may be received again or even frequently on successive days until death.

SEVEN

EUCHARISTIC RESERVATION AND ADORATION

61. Why do we reserve the Eucharist?

St. Justin Martyr (c. 150) describes the deacons at the end of the eucharistic celebration as taking the Eucharist to those who are absent—presumably the ill and imprisoned. Later this practice of reserving the sacrament in one's home was discontinued, but it was still reserved in the church building (often in the sacristy) for the ill and those not able to be at the celebration of the eucharistic sacrifice.

In some churches today after Communion at the principal Mass, ministers of Communion are sent forth with Communion from the eucharistic sacrifice for all of the ill and shut-ins, not only bringing them the Lord, but joining them to the celebration of the local church in their parish.

The document *Holy Communion and Eucharistic Worship Outside Mass* gives us the rationale for Eucharistic reservation:

> The primary and original reason for the reservation of the Eucharist outside Mass is the administration of viaticum. The secondary reasons are the giving of communion and the adoration of Our Lord Jesus Christ who is present in the sacrament. The reservation of the sacrament for the sick led to the praiseworthy custom of adoring the heavenly food in the churches. This cult of adoration rests on an authentic and solid basis, especially because faith in the real presence of the Lord leads naturally to external, public expression of faith. (no. 5)

62. What is Exposition of the Blessed Sacrament?

This is a medieval form of eucharistic devotion. In the Middle Ages the Mass was celebrated in Latin, whether sung at High Mass or read quietly as Low Mass, as was beginning to be the custom. After Berengar had been corrected for seeing the Eucharistic

Presence as only symbolic, the practice of elevating the host immediately after the consecration became very popular. This was taken up by the people since much of their participation in Mass at the time was visual or expressed in postures and of course in silent prayer. Popular piety even assigned various blessings to be received for looking on the host that day. Monstrances (from the Latin *monstrare,* "to show") and *ostensoria* (from the Latin *ostendere,* "to show") were vessels of precious metal made with a crystal tube or window so that the host could be seen and adored. A vessel of either type was sometimes taken out of the ambry or sacrament tower to bless the people, or the latter was often designed with open grill-work so that the host was visible all day.

The current rite of Exposition is viewed as a continuation or extension of the Mass. This is seen particularly in the rite for a solemn Exposition, when it is recommended that a host be consecrated at the Mass for Exposition, that after Communion it be placed in the monstrance and the concluding prayer be said but that no blessing or dismissal be given. The Mass is extended to the period of Exposition, and Benediction at the end of such adoration is the blessing and dismissal (HCEWOM).

63. What is Benediction of the Blessed Sacrament?

Exposition grew in response to the medieval desire to see the Blessed Sacrament and to adore Christ in this sacrament of the Eucharist. At the end of Vespers or Compline (Evening Prayer and Night Prayer respectively), which were well attended in religious-order churches and even parish churches, the priest at the end of the service would take out the Blessed Sacrament in the monstrance and the congregation would salute it with a hymn (hence the French term *salut* for Benediction of the Blessed Sacrament) and often salute the Blessed Virgin Mary with the "Salve Regina" or other Marian hymn. The priest would then bless the people with the Blessed Sacrament much like the bishop can bless the people with the Gospel Book at Mass. In the course of time Benediction became an independent ceremony in itself detached from the Liturgy of the Hours and, as has been said, became very popular in itself. Among Venerable John Henry Newman's sermons there is a lovely one describing evening devotions ending with Benediction, the Lord blessing his people at the end of the day, and Newman sees it as an enactment of the blessing from the Book of Numbers: "The LORD bless you and keep you; the LORD make his face to shine upon you, and be gracious to you; the LORD lift up his countenance upon you, and give you peace" (Num 6:24–26).

64. Aren't these medieval devotions somewhat passé in the era of the renewed eucharistic liturgy?

In 1972, shortly after the new Order of Mass was promulgated (1969), the document Holy Communion and Eucharistic Worship outside Mass (HCEWOM) was published, providing the guidelines and rubrics for Exposition and Benediction, giving these ceremonies a new setting and orientation: "The celebration of the Eucharist in the sacrifice of the Mass is the origin and consummation of the worship shown to the Eucharist outside Mass" (no. 2). Thus eucharistic worship is seen as an overflow of the Mass celebrated in the midst of and for the assembly, perhaps to assuage the fears of the liturgists who thought that eucharistic devotion would lead people away from the renewed Mass. The document continues in affirming Christ's continuing presence in the sacred species: "Reserved in our churches or oratories, he is in truth Emmanuel, i.e., 'God with us.' For he is in our midst day and night, he dwells in us full of grace and truth" (ibid.). The document then treats specifically of eucharistic devotion and reminds the faithful that by prayer before Christ in the Blessed Sacrament, "They prolong that union which they have achieved with him in Holy Communion and renew the covenant which commits them to practice in their lives and conduct what they have received in faith in the celebration of the Eucharist and in the reception of the Sacrament" (no. 81).

Here again we see eucharistic devotion—Exposition and Benediction as a prolongation of the Eucharist celebrated. This is fitting since the eucharistic mystery has so many facets that we can't contemplate them all at Mass: meal, sacrifice, presence, communion, memorial, liturgy, etcetera, so that it's good to have the contemplative atmosphere that eucharistic adoration provides to ponder the many aspects of this great mystery. John Paul II stated: "The Church and the world have great need of Eucharistic worship. Jesus awaits us in this sacrament of love. Let us not refuse the time to go and meet him in adoration, in contemplation, full of faith, and open to making amends for the serious offenses and crimes of the world. Let our adoration never cease" (D.C. 3, quoted in CCC no. 1380). Many seem to agree, if we can gauge the success of eucharistic adoration that is sweeping the country and the world. Youth 2000 is a highly successful youth retreat based around adoration. Many parishes have established daily or perpetual eucharistic adoration, and bishops have ordered it as a means for their dioceses to pray for vocations.

Personally I think silent adoration, gazing on the Eucharist surrounded by flickering candles, gives our prayer a focus. It helps people to see the mystical emphasis in Christian spirituality that is part of the Western heritage and need not be found only in the non-Christian East or in New Age practices. Also, I think it helps us rediscover the contemplative, transcendent dimensions of the liturgy itself that perhaps an overly activistic interpretation of participation overshadowed. The term for "active participation" in Latin is *actuosa* not *activa,* which is a perfectly good Latin word. That *actuosa* was chosen suggests that "real" or "actual" participation goes to the deepest activity of the mind and heart as well as external activities. While it is true that we worship the Father "in Spirit and truth" (John 4:24), the Word became incarnate and took our flesh, that is, became embodied. We believe that his Body is worthy of worship or adoration because it is conjoined to his divinity: one person in two natures. This is also true of Christ present in the Eucharist. Therefore we can say with Saint Augustine, "...not only do we not sin in adoring; rather we would sin if we did not" (In *Psalmum*, 98, 9).

Redemptionis Sacramentum highly recommends this practice of Exposition, but warns that the Blessed Sacrament must not be left unattended, even for the briefest space of time—at least one person should always be present (no. 138). It suggests that in cities one church be set aside for perpetual adoration (no. 140).

65. Isn't adoration something just for religious communities?

It is true that HCEWOM (no. 90) speaks of those religious communities who practice perpetual adoration or have adoration for long periods of time, and reminds them of the norms they should follow. The Congregation for Divine Worship does not see perpetual adoration as the normal thing for parish churches, but leaves the final decision in the hands of the local bishop (see *Solemn Exposition of the Holy Eucharist*, USCC, p. 37). Many bishops are following the lead of John Paul II, who, shortly after his election as pope, established daily eucharistic adoration in the four major basilicas in Rome directly under his care: Sts. Peter, Mary Major, John Lateran, and Paul Outside the Walls. These join the many downtown churches in Rome with daily Exposition. It is up to the bishop to decide when daily or perpetual adoration can be carried out with reverence and with sufficient numbers to adore so that the Blessed Sacrament is not left alone. Of course, adoration of the Blessed Sacrament does not require Exposition. Any visit before the tabernacle can be adoration.

The Holy Father in *Ecclesia de Eucharistia* encourages both eucharistic adoration and Exposition because "it is pleasant to spend time with Him, to lie close to his heart," for "how can we not feel a renewed need to spend time in spiritual converse, in silent adoration, in heartfelt love before Christ present in the Most Holy Sacrament?" (no. 25). The pope is recommending this prayer for all, not just religious.

66. What are some of the guidelines for eucharistic adoration according to HCEWOM?

The ordinary minister of exposition is the priest or a deacon. In his absence, an acolyte, extraordinary minister, or one appointed by the bishop may expose the Blessed Sacrament, that is, put it in the monstrance and place it on the altar, or bring the Eucharist to the altar if the tabernacle is not nearby. A eucharistic song may be sung ("O Salutaris" is the traditional favorite) while the Eucharist is incensed by the priest or deacon (other ministers do not incense). During the time of adoration readings, music, prayers, and a homily are all recommended to focus the attention of the faithful on the eucharistic mystery. One might note that in Roman churches this is rarely done. Praying some part of the Liturgy of the Hours is recommended as well. When this is done one has hymns, readings, prayers, and a possible homily, all of which are recommended, within the very structure of the Office. Silent prayer is much encouraged, and it would seem that this is much needed today. When the Exposition draws to a close (we're not talking of perpetual adoration), Benediction takes place. A eucharistic hymn is sung ("Tantum Ergo" is the traditional song) while the priest or deacon incenses the Blessed Sacrament. He sings or says the prayer, blesses the people with the Blessed Sacrament in the Sign of the Cross, and reposes the Eucharist in the tabernacle. The Divine Praises are no longer obligatory but are still permitted as an acclamation. A final hymn may be sung.

When entering and leaving the Eucharistic Presence a double genuflection is no longer required. Whether before the monstrance or tabernacle, a single genuflection suffices (no. 84).

67. May any prayer at all be said before the exposed Blessed Sacrament?

HCEWOM (no. 95) states that there should be prayers, songs, and readings (from Scripture) "to direct the attention of the Faithful to the worship of Christ the Lord." Since Christ is present in this sacrament of the altar, it would seem odd to have a public novena to St. Anthony before the Eucharist in the monstrance. The same would be true of prayers recited to Our Lady. Prayers, litanies, hymns, and chaplets to the Lord are appropriate, although attention should be given to the need for silence. Private prayers are left to one's discretion.

One might further ask if this applies to the Rosary. A response to this query in *Notitiae* (1968, 4) stated that since the Rosary is classified as a Marian prayer, it could not be recited publicly before the Blessed Sacrament exposed. We must note that although *Notitiae* is an organ of the Congregation for Divine Worship, *Notitiae's* responses are time conditioned and change. In 1974, Paul VI issued *Marialis Cultus,* in which he described the Rosary as a meditation on the paschal mystery, on the life, death, and resurrection of the Lord Jesus, which shows it is appropriate and sufficiently Christic to pray before the Eucharist. After John Paul II instituted daily Eucharist adoration in the four major basilicas of Rome, the Rosary was recited publicly in these holy places before the Blessed Sacrament exposed. Recently, the Congregation for Divine Worship has stated that the Rosary may be recited before the monstrance containing the Eucharist as long as the Eucharist was not exposed just to say the Rosary before it (*Notitiae* XXXIV [1998]: 501–11). *Redemptionis Sacramentum* calls the praying of the Rosary before the Blessed Sacrament admirable and praises the simplicity and profundity of this prayer (no. 137).

68. Are Corpus Christi or eucharistic processions still encouraged?

Corpus Christi, the feast of the Lord's Body and Blood, is celebrated on the Thursday or the Sunday (in the United States) after Trinity Sunday. This feast originated at the request of the visionary Juliana of Cornillon of the Bishop of Liege in 1246. In 1264 Pope Urban IV extended this feast to the whole Church, with Office and Mass composed by St. Thomas Aquinas (d. 1274), who selected the psalms, readings, *responsoria,* etcetera, from sacred Scripture, wrote hymns, and arranged the elements into a harmonious whole, both in the Mass and the Office (Liturgy of the Hours). The emphasis was not so much on the institution of the Eucharist or the unity in the Mystical Body that the Eucharist brings about, both of which are emphasized in the liturgy of Holy Thursday. Rather, the emphasis of St. Thomas in the Corpus Christi texts is the abiding presence of Christ in the Eucharist, although the texts from Scripture that he chose and the themes he wove into his hymns, "Pange Lingua," "Verbum Supernum Prodiens," "Lauda Sion," and "Adoro Te Devote," pretty much run the gamut, especially in terms of Old Testament types and New Testament fulfillment.

Corpus Christi became very popular in Europe, celebrated in France as Fétè Dieu. Carpets of flowers are laid, bands play and march in the outdoor procession after Mass, benedictions are given, and cannons shot off. This is still an important day in many parts of Europe, and recently bishops in the United States have reclaimed this custom. In the United States, the custom of having indoor processions developed because American Catholics were not always as public in proclaiming their eucharistic faith in a pluralistic society. A response to a query in *Notitiae* (II [1975]: 64) discourages indoor processions, but we have seen that although *Notitiae* is an organ of the Congregation for Divine Worship, the responses are not binding.

69. What is Forty Hours?

It seems to have begun in the early 1500s in Milan at the Church of the Holy Sepulchre as a commemoration of the forty hours the Lord's body lay in the tomb after its entombment and before the resurrection. It was recognized by Pope Clement VIII for the churches in Rome in 1592, and from Rome it spread to many other places. This devotion was first celebrated in this country in the Diocese of Baltimore in 1857 and was extended to the whole country by a decision of the Second Council of Baltimore in 1868.

Many of us can remember this devotion in our youth. Part of it was the celebration of Mass *Coram Sacratissimo* (before the Blessed Sacrament exposed), a practice now strictly forbidden (HCEWOM no. 83) as a conflict in meaning. Number 86 of HCEWOM seems to encourage Forty Hours or something like it in recommending "a period of solemn exposition of the Blessed Sacrament every year" in churches and oratories (no. 86). The contemporary movement Youth 2000 is an updated version of Forty Hours presented in a way to attract youth; it is very successful.

70. What is a eucharistic congress?

Eucharistic congresses for promoting devotion to the Blessed Sacrament began on a local level. The idea for such a congress came from Marie Tamisier, a laywoman who confided her desire to honor the Eucharist in this way to her confessor, St. Peter Julian Eymard, founder of the Blessed Sacrament Fathers, who encouraged her. In 1881 in Lille, her bishop, Msgr. Gaston de Ségur, presided over eight thousand people gathered together to honor Christ's presence in the Blessed Sacrament. It was a great success, and Pope Leo XIII endorsed the idea; since then, congresses have been held all over the world in the last century: London, Chicago, Philadelphia, Manila, Delhi, and Rome for the millennium jubilee. The document HCEWOM has a section on eucharistic congresses, which it sees as a kind of "station," *statio,* for the local sponsoring church inviting the Church elsewhere to "join in the deepest profession of some aspect of the eucharistic mystery and express their worship publicly in the bond of charity and unity. Such congresses should be a genuine sign of faith and charity by reason of the total participation of the local Church and the association with it of the other Churches" (no. 109).

Studies beforehand are recommended in preparation for a thorough catechesis for different groups at the congress on the meaning of the Eucharist, such as, how to enter into the mystery and how to relate this to temporal concerns and social justice as well (nos. 110, 111).

Finally, as one would expect, the celebration of the Eucharist should be the apex of the congress; the given theme should be explored in devotional services, catechetical meetings, and public conferences; common prayer and eucharistic adoration should be planned; and any public processions should follow ecclesial regulations while still respecting and observing any local traditions (no. 112).

71. What is said about the Eucharist in the Code of Canon Law?

Canons 897 through 958 cover all different aspects of the Eucharist. We see the Eucharist described as a sacrifice that perpetuates the sacrifice of the cross and therefore is the summit and source of worship (897). It is to be celebrated in faith, received frequently, and worshiped (898) because in it Christ is substantially present under the species of bread and wine (899). The minister of this sacrament, a validly ordained priest (900), can offer this sacrifice for both the living and the dead (901). He may celebrate Mass individually or concelebrate with other Catholic priests (901), but may not concelebrate with non-Catholic clergy (908). At Mass, only the priest says the Eucharistic Prayer (907), although others may assume other roles. Though others may help distribute Communion as extraordinary ministers when there is need, the ordinary minister of the Eucharist is the bishop, the priest, or the deacon (910). The priest is encouraged to celebrate Mass frequently (904) and, for pastoral need, the bishop may allow him to binate (celebrate twice) on weekdays or trinate (celebrate three times) on Sundays (905). Only the baptized can be admitted to

Communion (912), and children who are well prepared and have sufficient knowledge may receive (913) at the age of reason (914). Those excommunicated or interdicted may not receive except in danger of death (915). Those guilty of grave sin must confess before receiving unless there is a grave reason and there is no opportunity to confess, in which case they are to make a perfect act of contrition and resolve to go to confession as soon as possible (916). All must fast for an hour from solid food and all liquids (except water) before receiving Communion. However, medicine is not considered food, and this law does not bind the old and the ill and those who are actually caring for them (919). All Catholics must receive Communion at least once a year during the Easter season (920) and may always receive in any Catholic rite, even if not their own (923), and may receive under one species or both (925). Viaticum for the dying should not be delayed (922). Latin-Rite Catholics receive under the species of unleavened bread (926), and their Masses are either in Latin or another approved vernacular (928). For Mass, priests should wear the appropriate vestments (929) and celebrate the Eucharist in a church on an altar or, if necessary, in a decent place on a suitable table (932). The Blessed Sacrament should be reserved in the church or chapel (934), and such should be open for the veneration and prayer of the faithful (937). Ordinarily there should be one tabernacle in a church, immovable, solid, and opaque, and locked, so there is no danger of desecration (938). The tabernacle should be placed in a distinguished, conspicuous, beautifully decorated location or chapel that is suitable for prayer (ibid.). There should always be a lamp burning near the tabernacle to show the presence of Christ (940). Exposition of the Blessed Sacrament is permitted, but not at the same time as Mass in the same area (942), and the custom of a solemn annual exposition (Forty Hours) is encouraged (943). Canons 943 through 958 deal with the monetary offerings for Masses, called stipends.

72. What are the major documents on the Eucharist issued since Vatican II?

Sacrosanctum Concilium (the Constitution on the Sacred Liturgy), issued in 1963, was the watershed document of Vatican II, laying down the principles of renewal and restoration of the sacred liturgy and the Mass, and *Inter Oecumenici* (1964) was the document that explained how these principles were to be implemented. Pope Paul VI, concerned over misinterpretations of eucharistic doctrine, issued *Mysterium Fidei* in 1965 as a corrective, and *Eucharisticum Mysterium* followed in 1967 as the Congregation of Rites buttressed the same teaching on the sacrificial dimension of the Mass and the Real Presence as well, later that same year. *Musicam Sacram,* also issued in 1967, laid down the principles of sacred music for the Roman Church, trusting local hierarchies to adapt the principles to their cultures. In 1969 the new *Ordo Missae* (Order of Mass), with four new Eucharistic Prayers, and *Lectionary* were issued in Latin, and in English the following year. Accompanying that was the General Instruction of the Roman Missal (GIRM) with the rubrical guidelines for the present Mass; the GIRM was reissued in 1975 and again in 2002. In 1973 guidelines for Masses with children were promulgated, and new Eucharistic Prayers were introduced for them. The Liturgy of the Hours with its general instruction was promulgated in 1975. *Memoriale Domini* permitted Communion in the hand as an option in 1976. John Paul II, in 1980, early on in his pontificate, gave us a glimpse of his approach to the eucharistic doctrine of the Church and its centrality in *Dominicae Cenae,* and it was followed by *Inestimabile Donum* of the Congregation of Divine Worship, dealing with problems and abuses, that same year. In 2003 *Ecclesia de Eucharistia* filled out the Holy Father's eucharistic teaching, and was followed by a document of the Congregation for Divine Worship, *Redemptionis Sacramentum,* which deals with abuses that "contribute to the obscuring of the Catholic faith and doctrine concerning this wonderful sacrament" (no. 6).

EIGHT

THE ARCHITECTURE AND VESSELS
OF EUCHARISTIC RESERVATION

73. What is a tabernacle? What are its requirements?

The tabernacle is named for the tent or *tabernaculum* (Latin), which was erected in the desert to shelter the Ark of the Covenant over which God's presence or *Shekinah* (Hebrew) dwelt as God led the Hebrews through the desert (cf. Exod 25:10). The modern Catholic tabernacle dates from the time of the Renaissance or early Counter-Reformation period, when reservation of the eucharistic species was placed in a boxlike or circular cupboard on the high altar by the Dominicans in Florence, a practice later recommended by St. Charles Borromeo in Milan. If Catholic teaching of Christ's presence in the Eucharist was denied in the Protestant north, then Catholics would affirm it with a vengeance in the Catholic south by placing it in the most prominent spot in the Church, on the high altar. It is no longer required that the tabernacle be on the high altar, or on an altar at all. In fact the Blessed Sacrament should not be reserved on an altar on which Mass is celebrated (GIRM no. 315). Many different approaches to reservation are allowed as long as the Blessed Sacrament is reserved in a conspicuous place (cf. GIRM 314). The tabernacle itself should be "immovable, made of solid and unbreakable material and not transparent and locked so that the danger of desecration is avoided as much as possible" (ibid.; cf. canon 938).

74. Where is the tabernacle placed in a Catholic church?

To answer that question adequately, we must look at the directions for the ordering of the church structure that the Church lays down. The General Instruction describes the church and particularly the sanctuary in terms of the sacred synaxis, or assembly of the faithful who gather for the Eucharist. It treats first the altar; next the ambo, or lectern for the Word; then the chair for the priest celebrant; the places of the people and choir; and then the place

for the reservation of the Eucharist. It seems that the first concern
of the document is to give pride of place to the Eucharist as it is
being celebrated, and then to the Eucharist as the Body of the
Lord being reserved for the ill, for Viaticum, and for devotions,
namely, both communal and individual prayer.

It is interesting to note that the *Catechism* seems to see the
tabernacle as an extension of the altar in that it treats of it just
after the discussion of the altar and before those of the chair and
ambo (lectern). It is clear that where the consecrated species is
kept is a very important question, and more recent legislation is
more open to different possibilities than perhaps the stricter interpretation that dominated just after the council. Ultimately the
decision of the local bishop prevails (cf. GIRM 315), and he
decides whether the Eucharist is reserved in the sanctuary (the
tabernacle is not usually on an altar) or in a separate eucharistic
chapel. In any case the tabernacle ought to be in a part of the
church that is "noble, worthy, conspicuous, well decorated and
suitable for prayer" (GIRM 314).

75. What is a eucharistic-reservation Chapel?

The 1970 General Instruction seemed to give pride of place
to a separate eucharistic chapel, which was a very common feature of European cathedrals and basilicas. It stated, "It is strongly
recommended that the Blessed Sacrament be reserved in a special
chapel well suited for private adoration and prayer apart from the
nave. But if the plan of the church or legitimate local custom
impedes this, then the Sacrament should be kept on an altar or
elsewhere in the church in a place of honor suitably adorned" (no.
276). Except for some cathedrals in this country, the former custom was always to have the tabernacle on the main altar in the
sanctuary. Possibly recognizing "legitimate local custom" or the
unworthy solution to reserving the Blessed Sacrament in an
alcove, where the congregation had its back to it, or even in a separate building, the new General Instruction, while still giving the

option of a separate chapel for adoration and prayer, lists reservation in the sanctuary first (no. 315), which would make sense for most parish churches. Chapels make sense in cathedrals, heavily visited historic or artistic churches filled with tourists, so that there is a quiet place for the faithful to pray before the Blessed Sacrament. It should be beautifully decorated with eucharistic themes and easily seen from the main body of the church as *Built of Living Stones* mandates (nos. 73, 77).

76. What is the history of reserving the Eucharist?

The Eucharist was reserved first for the ill and the dying because of the Catholic beliefs that the consecrated bread remains the Body of the Lord and that both the sick and the dying need Communion. From earliest times it was the custom to reserve the Eucharist for the ill, as we've seen in the writings of St. Justin in the second century. St. Cyprian of Carthage (d. 258) describes reservation in private homes for daily reception of Communion because the liturgy was only celebrated on Sundays. But as the *Catechism* states: "As faith in the Real Presence of Christ in his Eucharist deepened the Church became conscious of the meaning of silent adoration of the Lord present under the Eucharistic species" (no. 1379). As this happened, then reserving the Eucharist (or the Blessed Sacrament, as it began to be called) in the sacristy did not seem sufficient, so wall ambries or aumbries (wall cupboards) were fashioned for the sanctuaries of churches (e.g., a tenth-century one in the ancient basilica of San Clemente in Rome). As the Middle Ages progressed, new creative ways were found to reserve the Blessed Sacrament: sometimes in a vessel suspended over the altar—a metal dove with a place within to keep the Eucharist—or in the late medieval period, a tower alongside the altar. Finally the custom was to reserve the sacred species in a tabernacle on the central altar, where increasingly adoration took the forms of Exposition and Benediction.

77. What ways may the Blessed Sacrament be reserved now?

We have already considered various ways that the Blessed
Sacrament has been reserved in history, and many of these ways
are being rediscovered. Wall cupboards or ambries are being
used. Some in Italy are designed in such wise that, set in a wall in
the sanctuary, when the doors are open, the Blessed Sacrament is
placed in an inner door, all ready for adoration. Sacrament towers
are again being built, or a tabernacle is often placed on a pillar or
stand. The Cathedral of Killarney in Ireland, originally designed
by A. W. Pugin, now has a very impressive "sacrament tower"
that dominates its simplified interior. Eucharistic doves suspended over the altar are used in some Byzantine sanctuaries, as
well as in the Roman Rite (albeit rarely).

The General Instruction states that it is "more in keeping
with its meaning as a sign that the tabernacle in which the Most
Blessed Sacrament is reserved not be on the altar where Mass is
celebrated" (315). However, further on it states that apart from the
altar of celebration, "an old altar which is no longer used for celebration" is not excluded (ibid.). It would seem to me that in
many an old church, where the high altar, in Gothic, Renaissance,
Baroque, or some other revivalist style dominated the central axis
of the church and where the architecture would be destroyed by
removing it (as, alas, has happened in many places), then the old
altar can be an appropriate place of reservation and that a new
center of liturgical gravity can be created closer to the people for
the altar of celebration. When Mass is celebrated the focus is on
the altar, but otherwise, the focus is on the tabernacle.

78. What are the major eucharistic vessels?

For the celebration of Mass, the primary vessels are the cup
or chalice for the wine and the paten or flat dish for the eucharistic bread or host. The chalice is mentioned in all the Synoptic
Gospels and by St. Paul (1 Cor 10:16; 11:25, 28), and a plate or
dish for the bread is implied. The earliest plates or patens were

large enough to hold the loaf to be broken for many, but as individual hosts began to be made (early medieval period), a special vessel called a ciborium was used for them, and the paten for the priest's host was small and rather flat and designed so it fit on top of the chalice. The ciborium often has a stem or little pedestal like the chalice, and a lid, and the hosts left over after Mass are placed in it and reposed in the tabernacle. The General Instruction allows the use of a larger paten, often with sides, to hold a larger host to be broken as well as individual hosts (no. 331). The more frequent use of Communion under both species often meant that a flagon or pitcher was placed on the altar with the wine to be consecrated, which was later poured into separate chalices to be used for the people's Communion. The use of a flagon is no longer allowed by *Redemptionis Sacramentum,* at least in terms of consecrating the wine in it. While wine may be brought to the altar in a flagon, it should be poured into as many chalices as will be needed during the preparation of the gifts, so that there is no danger of spilling the consecrated species while pouring it into chalices after consecration (cf. no. 106).

The General Instruction mandates that sacred vessels be made of noble metal and that if they are not gold then they be gold plated inside to avoid rust (no. 328). Bishop's conferences are given the option of allowing other solid materials to be used if they are considered noble (e.g., ebony) and are not easily breakable (no. 327). This would seem to rule out glass. Chalices in particular are to be made of nonabsorbent material, or at least the actual cup portion (no. 330). The sacred vessels should be clearly distinguished from items intended for everyday use (no. 322).

79. What is a pyx? What is a monstrance or ostensorium?

A pyx is a small, flat, usually circular box that holds one or several hosts. A very small pyx looking somewhat like a pocket watch is used to carry Communion to the ill and can be carried in a breast pocket. A pyx is used for the *lunette,* or circular framed glass vessel that holds the host for Exposition of the Blessed Sacrament. A pyx in Christian antiquity was the small box used to bring the Eucharist from the Sunday celebration to the Christian home for daily Communion of the sacred species reserved in this vessel.

A monstrance is a stand often made of precious metal, which is a display case made of glass and lined with gold to show the sacred host for adoration. From this it receives its name — in Latin *monstrare* means "to show." Often the design of the monstrance is a sunburst, which became popular in the Baroque period. Since Christ is the Light of the World (cf. John 8:12) or the Sun of Righteousness (cf. Mal 3:20), it seems appropriate to so encase the Blessed Sacrament. Sometimes the case will be more Gothic, with spires and statues of saints, like a little Gothic cathedral. This vessel for exposition is also called an ostensorium from another Latin word, *ostendere,* also meaning "to show."

80. How are these vessels blessed for use in the liturgy?

It was necessary in the old rite to have chalices and patens blessed by the bishop. Now a priest may bless these objects as well. The *Book of Blessings* situates the blessing of these vessels within Mass, and after the Prayer of the Faithful they are blessed with a prayer (no. 1369). After bread and wine are brought to the altar in procession, the bread and wine are put into these vessels, which are offered in the usual way (no. 1370), and the Mass proceeds as usual. These vessels may also be blessed with a Liturgy of the Word if Mass is not advisable (cf. nos. 1373–87). Ciboria, monstrances, pyxes, vestments, altar cloths, corporals (small square cloths put directly under the eucharistic vessels at Mass or Exposition), missals (sacramentaries), and lectionaries may be blessed within Mass (cf. nos. 1347–59) or with a shorter rite (cf. nos. 1354–59).

81. What is the proper way to purify the sacred vessels?

The General Instruction gives the directions as to how the vessels are to be purified. Those responsible for such cleansing are the priest, the deacon, or the instituted acolyte, who cleanse the vessels after communion or after Mass, preferably at a side table (no. 279). In the United States ministers of Communion may also purify according to a rescript granted by the Holy See. The paten is usually wiped with the purificator so that any crumbs are brushed into the chalice(s) and the same is true of the ciborium. The chalice(s) are then cleansed by pouring water, or wine and water, into the chalice(s) and that is drunk by the one purifying. If any of the Precious Blood remains after Communion, it is completely consumed at the altar; it is not reserved (ibid). If hosts or particles of hosts should fall, they should be reverently retrieved. If any of the Precious Blood is spilled, the area where the spill occurred should be washed and the water poured into the sacrarium (no. 280). The sacrarium is a sink whose drain goes directly into the ground. The water from cleansing vessels (see above) or linens may be poured into such a sink, which should be provided in every sacristy (no. 334). The vessels may be purified during the Mass as is often done on weekdays.

NINE

EUCHARISTIC SPIRITUALITY

82. What is eucharistic spirituality? Is it a devotion? Is it biblical?

As we have seen, the Eucharist is the summit and the source of the life of the Church within the context of the liturgy. Clearly one's Christian life, one's way of prayer flows from the Eucharist. Thus it is a spirituality, not simply a "devotion," as the term has come to be understood—an optional form of prayer to which one is especially drawn. Devotions are popular nonliturgical prayers (often private) that are warmly recommended by the Church (cf. S.C. no. 13) if they are in conformity with the teaching of the Church. One can see that while eucharistic adoration is popular ("of the people") as an extension of the Mass, offering oneself in union with Christ's sacrifice, it goes beyond merely private or individual prayer, although eucharistic prayer is clearly a part of such a spirituality.

My elder brother, St. Thomas Aquinas, sees devotion as promptness of the will concerning the things of God, and in this sense if one loves the Mass and the Blessed Sacrament (whether exposed or in the tabernacle) one can be said to have a eucharistic piety or devotion. Father Vincent McNabb, the great English Dominican, said, "…those who love God quickly become eucharistic…," and thus they mold their spirituality on the Eucharist.

All Catholics are called to worship God eucharistically or liturgically in the Mass and to receive the Lord in the Eucharist: "…unless you eat the flesh of the Son of Man and drink his blood, you have no life in you" (John 6:53). If Christ lives in us through the Eucharist and his sacrifice is made present in the Eucharist— "As often as you eat this bread and drink this cup, you proclaim the Lord's death until he comes…" (1 Cor. 11:26)—then the core of the Christian life as seen in the Gospel is eucharistic, and this spirituality is thoroughly biblical.

83. Is eucharistic spirituality trinitarian?

As we have seen before, the Eucharist is the sacrificial meal in which the Lord Jesus is made present in his paschal mystery, his saving death and resurrection. As he once offered himself on the cross as the new Adam, as the head of the new human race, that offering is made present again so we can enter in and offer ourselves to the Father. According to the *Constitution on the Sacred Liturgy,* the liturgy's role is the glorification of God and the sanctification of us, the Church gathered in his name (no. 7). The *Catechism* sees the Father as the source and goal of liturgy (no. 1077 ff.). He is the source of all as generating the Word, his Son, and creating all in him in unity with the Spirit. Our glorification of God is recognizing that all comes from him. We do not praise him for his good but for ours, to remind ourselves of the order of the universe. As C. S. Lewis put it, "Praise is mental health made audible." Our praise goes to the Father through Jesus Christ, the mediator between God and man. As the new Adam, the head of the new human race, he can offer perfect praise for us, and as God he can bring the Divine Spirit and his gifts of grace and goodness.

Because Christ is made present in the Mass in ways that we have explored before, he is able to sanctify us through the Spirit. The *Catechism* sees the Spirit as sanctifying us by preparing us to encounter the Lord in the Word (no. 1093). The Holy Spirit also "recalls" the events of salvation history, especially the death and resurrection of Christ, and makes this mystery sacramentally present, so that we can receive him into our hearts, our minds, our lives (cf. no. 1104 ff.).

Finally, as Jungmann would remind us, the shape of the Collect of the Roman Rite is the pattern of our prayer. All of the classic Collects begin by addressing God the Father, *ad Patrem,* calling him "God" or "Father." The body of the prayer concludes through the mediatorship of Jesus Christ, *per Filium ejus Jesum Christum* and in the unity of the Holy Spirit *in Spiritu Sancto.* That is the pattern ultimately of all prayer, the pattern of the

Eucharist and that of Christian spirituality, although different emphases may be given by different people or schools of thought.

John Paul II in *Ecclesia de Eucharistia* reminded us that the Lord said, "As the living Father sent me and I live because of the Father, so he who eats me will live because of me" (John 6:57). He continued, "Jesus reassures us that this union, which he compares to that of the life of the Trinity, is truly realized" (no. 16). So our union with Christ in the Eucharist mirrors the inner unity of Father, Son, and Holy Spirit.

84. Is eucharistic spirituality Charismatic? Is it the work of the Holy Spirit?

The Charismatic Renewal is a movement in the Catholic Church that began after John XXIII had asked the whole Church to pray for "a new Pentecost." Among the new initiatives of the council was a new openness to other churches and ecclesial communities. Pentecostalism had sprung from the Holiness movement in some Protestant traditions and had resurfaced in the mainline Protestant communities in the early '60s. What was new in this spiritual movement was a belief that the Charismatic gifts outlined by St. Paul in his First Letter to the Corinthians (ch. 12) were not simply phenomena for the apostolic Church but are still experienced today (cf. CCC nos. 799–801). The most controversial of these gifts is the gift of tongues (cf. 1 Cor 14), experienced not so much as a way of communication (although, coupled with the gifts of prophecy and interpretation, that often happens) but as a gift of prayer, as a nonlinguistic, preconceptional way of praying, akin to jubilation in the early Church, Gregorian chant, or the rhythm of the Rosary or litanies. As Charismatics experienced this mode of prayer in their very exuberant prayer meetings, they later frequently tended to be drawn to quiet prayer before the tabernacle and toward eucharistic adoration. So, while this Charismatic approach to prayer is indeed very different from the deep silence of eucharistic adoration, in the lives of many, the one leads them to the other. Of course all of this is the work of the Holy Spirit.

We saw in question 19 the role of the *Epiclesis,* the prayer calling down the Holy Spirit in the Eucharistic Prayer before the Consecration, praying that the Spirit would change the elements into the Body and Blood of Christ, and another *Epiclesis* after the Consecration, praying that the Spirit would transform us consuming the sacramental Body of Christ more and more into the mystical Body of Christ, the Church. Theology teaches us that while all the works of the Holy Trinity *ad extra* (outside of the inner workings of the trinitarian life) are done by the Godhead, still the work of creation is attributed to the Father, of redemption to the Son, and of sanctification to the Spirit because this is the way they are presented in the Bible. The *Catechism* sees the Spirit as sanctifying us in preparing us to experience the "memorial" of the Lord's death and resurrection that the Spirit "recalls" (nos. 1091–1109). But it is the same Spirit who acts individually in our souls, sanctifying them by the gifts of the Spirit and collectively and liturgically in the Church. Although the Spirit always acts with and through the Church, it is not bound to the Church alone, but acts with great variety.

85. Are service of the poor and social justice opposed to eucharistic spirituality?

The stereotype would pit very ritualistic clerics with high collars executing very "high church" liturgies against those slugging it out "in the trenches" in slum neighborhoods, attending very free-wheeling Masses or perhaps not at all. People who are truly Catholic know that they must have the Eucharist, that they need the Lord: both his Word and his Body that they receive at the Eucharist, and also that they must seek his face in the poor, "for…just as you did…to the least of these who are members of my family, you did it to me" (Matt 25:40).

One thinks of Dorothy Day, the founder of the Catholic Worker movement with Peter Maurin, who tried not only to help the poor but to change society's approach to government, economics, war and peace, and found great solace in Mass and the liturgy of the Church. In the early days of her movement, she had chant instructors teach the Catholic Worker staff Gregorian Mass chants and how to pray hours of the Divine Office together. She was always grateful to Cardinal Spellman, with whose position she violently disagreed on the war in Vietnam, because he allowed her to keep the Blessed Sacrament at St. Joseph's on Christie Street. One also thinks of Catherine Doherty, founder of Madonna House, a lay apostolate movement, long before the lay apostolate was much encouraged, and Friendship House, an interracial apostolate, before blacks and whites encountered one another in an atmosphere of friendship. A quotation attributed to her shows her great love of the Eucharist and need for it: "I can bear anything between two Masses." The example of these women shows that true eucharistic piety and love of the Mass and service of the poor cannot be divorced from one another. Indeed, they call out to each other.

Of course the modern example for us in this time is Blessed Teresa of Calcutta. In her life we see no contradiction between service of the poor and love of the Eucharist. Mother Teresa's eucharistic spirituality evolved out of her own spiritual growth, and she in turn formed her followers, the Missionaries of Charity, in that same spirituality. In all convents of the Missionaries, by the crucifix behind the altar is written the legend "I thirst" (cf. John 19:28). This is seen as the total gift of God's thirst for us expressed in the Eucharist as the sacrament that thirsts for us, and our response to this love. In the sacrament of love, God desires union with us (with me), and that union transforms me, so that all that is human in me as an individual is made divine. The transformation goes further and transforms the many individuals into one in Christ, the Father's great gift to us in this sacrifice. And in him, we thirst for God and for others to know God. God's life in us calls out to others so that they might be filled with God's life. The holy mysteries of his Body and Blood that begin each day in the convent are the way the Missionaries praise God so that their work and life might echo that praise, so that they might be an extension of God's love, service, and charity. Mother Teresa taught her sisters to see Christ in the golden chalice and paten on the altar and then in the dying on the street. If one is transformed by the eucharistic Lord (for whom gold vessels are appropriate), then one will see him in the vessels of his Mystical Body as well. As the bread is broken, as Christ was broken on the cross, so is the Missionary to be broken in service to the poor. They become the bread of mercy to the poor. They become what they celebrate and are able to contemplate this mystery each evening in the holy hour before the end of the day. This sums up how Mother Teresa's approach to the Eucharist shaped her life of service to the poorest of the poor.

She realized that in "a globalized world where the weakest, the most powerless and the poorest appear to have so little hope…the Lord wished to remain with us in the Eucharist, making his presence in meal and sacrifice the promise of a humanity renewed by this love" (E. E. no. 20).

86. What was Pope John Paul's eucharistic spirituality?

In *Redemptor Hominis,* John Paul II's first of many instructions to the Church and the world in many forms, the pope spoke of the centrality of the Eucharist and called it a presence sacrament, a sacrifice sacrament, and a communion sacrament. It would seem that all his later teaching developed these themes.

John Paul taught us that at the Last Supper began a new presence of Christ for all the world, a presence that "constantly occurs whenever the Eucharist is celebrated and a priest lends his voice to Christ, repeating the sacred words of institution" (Holy Thursday Letter, 2000). By them God's glory shines forth in Christ in the Eucharist, for it is "the principal expression of Christ's presence among us" (speech at the papal audience,

September 27, 2000). To be present at a papal Mass celebrated by John Paul, whether with a vast assemblage at World Youth Day or in his private chapel (and I did both), was to be very much aware of how deeply open to and conscious of the Divine Presence, the personal presence of Jesus Christ, the pope was.

This memorial of the cross, the sacrifice on Calvary, is the heart of the Eucharist, "...which proclaims and celebrates the death and resurrection of Christ until he comes again is...the heart of the church's life" (Holy Thursday Letter, 2000). And again, "...come and see, in the Cross, you will see the radiant sign of the world's redemption, the loving presence of the living God" (World Youth Day Homily, 1997). The priest's task is to make this memorial present: "I have repeated these sacramental words in order to make Christ present, under the species of bread and wine, in the saving act of his self-sacrifice on the Cross" (Holy Thursday Letter, 1997). The pope then proceeded to instruct priests to live their lives in conformity with this sacrifice in their sacrificial living.

The Holy Father taught as well that the Eucharist, which is "the sacrifice which makes present the saving power of the cross," is also the "banquet of communion" (Homily at the Cenacle in Jerusalem, April 6, 2000). The Eucharist "as our sharing in the Body and Blood of Christ is also a mystery of spiritual communion in the Church....Through the Eucharist Christ builds up the Church. The hands that broke bread for the disciples at the Last Supper were to be stretched out on the cross in order to gather all people to himself in the eternal kingdom of his Father. Through the celebration of the Eucharist, he never ceases to draw men and women to be effective members of his body."

These are some of the key themes in the teaching of John Paul II on the Eucharist, which he clearly lived and prayed. We know this not only from personal experience from attendance at his Masses and hearing his homilies, but also from numerous anecdotes of his piety and reverence in the presence of the Blessed Sacrament engaged in personal prayer. I saw his rapt

attention before the Eucharistic Presence in his oratory, praying
before morning Mass began.

87. What are some of the key points that John Paul emphasized in *Ecclesia de Eucharistia?*

To celebrate his twenty-fifth anniversary as pope, John Paul
II issued his fourteenth encyclical, in place of his usual Holy
Thursday letter to priests, on the Eucharist—*Ecclesia de
Eucharistia.* No new doctrinal formulations are given, no new
dogmas are proclaimed, but the tradition is often cast in a new
light, a gift the Holy Father had, and he did not disappoint us in
this encyclical letter. His own personalistic approach and what the
Eucharist meant to him personally shine out in this document.

The theme is that the Eucharist flows from the paschal mystery, from the whole of the Triduum, and that the Church flows
from this *mysterium eucharisticum,* this *mysterium paschale* (no.
2). Holy Thursday and the institution of the Eucharist (which the
Holy Father proclaimed as the last luminous mystery of the
Rosary) was celebrated in light of the death on the cross on Good
Friday and yet also in light of the resurrection from the dead on
Easter Sunday, and so the Church sings, "…the Lord is risen from
the tomb; for our sake he hung upon the Cross, Alleluia" (cf. nos.
3, 4). The Church flows from this paschal mystery of the
Triduum: "Her foundation and wellspring is the whole Triduum
paschale, but this is as it were gathered up, foreshadowed and
'concentrated' for ever in the gift of the Eucharist" (no. 5).

At Mass the Church becomes the Body of Christ, fed on the
sacramental Body of Christ, because the priest "puts his voice at
the disposal of the One who spoke these words in the Upper
Room," so that Christ speaks through him (no. 5).

The pope remembered celebrating Mass in the Cenacle or
Upper Room, during his first assignment in the parish church of
Niegowic, the university church of St. Florian in Cracow, as pope
at St. Peter's and the other ancient basilicas of Rome, and through-

out the world. He spoke of celebrating in chapels built on mountain paths, on lakeshores and seacoasts, in stadiums and city squares (no. 8), and these various celebrations gave him an experience of the cosmic dimension of the Mass, its universality. Even if celebrated on a "humble altar of a country church," it is celebrated "on the altar of the World." It is cosmic because it is the "sacramental re-presentation" of the sacrifice of the cross; "…it is the sacrifice of the Cross perpetuated down the ages" (no. 11), and the cross is the center of all history, the center of the cosmos.

The Holy Father emphasized this teaching because some, he thought, strip the Eucharist of its sacrificial meaning and celebrate it "as if it were simply a fraternal banquet" (no. 11) without the necessity of priesthood rooted in apostolic succession, with the result that unsound ecumenical practices are initiated (ibid.). Consequently the dogmatic teaching creatively reiterates Trent on the sacrifice of the Mass as the same as that of the cross — a "commemorative representation" *(memorialis representatio)* (no. 16). Transubstantiation is also stressed (no. 15) so that our Communion is truly Christ's Body and Blood, and he quoted John 6:55: "My flesh is food indeed and my blood is drink indeed."

As the title suggests, the Church comes from the Eucharist: *Ecclesia de Eucharistia*. The pope drew from many strands of Scripture to make this point: from the twelve apostles (the seeds of the new Israel) and the beginning of the hierarchy to the sealing of the Old Covenant on Mount Sinai and that of the New on Mt. Calvary to our baptism in Christ, which points us toward the eucharistic sacrifice and communion in it (nos. 21–23). We are the many grains in the one loaf: "…the bread which we break, is it not a communion in the Body of Christ? Because there is one bread, we who are many are one body, for we all partake of the one bread" (1 Cor 10:16–17). Fed on the Body of Christ, we become the Mystical Body of Christ. That this happens requires the continuity and power of the mandate the Lord gave the apostles when he said, "Do this in remembrance of Me" (1 Cor 11:24), and so apostolic succession is key and fullness of Communion requires it.

Limited Communion can be permitted in certain circumstances (cf. qq. 54–59 in this book). A rich theology of Communion is given.

The pope concluded his encyclical with a fervent plea for reverence, beauty, and dignity in the celebration of the Liturgy of the Eucharist. Though it is a banquet, it is a heavenly banquet. Rather the *panis angelorum,* the bread of angels, has inspired "architecture, sculpture, painting and music, moved by the Christian mystery" (no. 49). "The Eucharist, while shaping the Church and her spirituality, has also powerfully affected 'culture' and the arts in particular" (ibid.). These are some highlights of this encyclical.

88. Are some religious orders devoted to eucharistic adoration?

The Lord Jesus appeared to St. Margaret Mary Alacoque as the Sacred Heart while she was at eucharistic adoration. In that era (seventeenth century) many cloistered communities of nuns took up the practice of eucharistic adoration (often perpetual). It became the calling of many older women's communities, for example, the Poor Clares and the Dominican order of nuns, as well as some communities of religious women founded in the nineteenth century. Most communities of men did not follow suit except the Blessed Sacrament Fathers, whose task it was to promote such adoration among the laity.

After Vatican II, many new orders sprang up in France and Italy and later in the United States. Some of these orders have Charismatic roots, that is they sprang out of Charismatic lay communities or were founded upon specifically Charismatic principles (e.g., the Beatitudes and Emmanuel). Some new communities had more of a monastic inspiration (e.g., the Brothers and Sisters of St. John), and many were an interesting mix of single laypeople, religious, married couples with families, and priests. Most of the new communities formed after the council have a deep ecclesial spirit that is expressed in a great love for the role of Peter, that is, the pope. They tend to have a tender devotion to the Blessed Virgin, and practically all of them observe some form of eucharistic devotion expressed in Exposition. While some may practice perpetual adoration, it is more common to have a period of Exposition following morning prayer, evening prayer, or both, or perhaps a daily holy hour; but unlike holy hours of the past, the great emphasis is on silent prayer, and as we have said before, the Blessed Sacrament exposed provides the atmosphere for an incarnational contemplation that these new groups cherish.

89. What is a holy hour?

A holy hour is an hour of prayer and devotion before the Blessed Sacrament exposed. In question 66 we outlined the Church's recommendations in terms of what is appropriate for eucharistic adoration: readings, songs, prayers, a homily, but all focused on the sacramental presence of the Lord. In the years prior to Vatican II, most holy hours included devotional prayers that focused on Christ present, but some were not always so oriented. Consecrations and other prayers to Our Lady or the saints, for example, while praiseworthy in themselves, ought not to be recited within the hour of adoration, although they might be fitting either before or after. In a holy hour, all should focus on Christ, as does the Office, along with those Scriptures chosen to be read, songs sung, and any Christological prayers, litanies, consecrations, etcetera. Silence is so needed now, that surely it should predominate to allow all to open their hearts to the Lord in the sacrament of the altar. How one prays in silence is of course an individual choice, and one must follow the lead of the Holy Spirit.

90. How does one pray in adoration before the Blessed Sacrament?

Since the Eucharist makes Christ present in the paschal mystery and since in the Rosary one meditates on the paschal mystery in devout recollection of various aspects of that mystery, as Pope Paul VI stated in *Marialis Cultis* (no. 42 ff.), then the Rosary is one excellent way to pray in adoration, especially since one of the new luminous mysteries proposed by Pope John Paul II in his *Rosarium Virginis Mariae* is the very institution of the Eucharist. He saw the Rosary as gazing on the face of Christ shining as the sun (cf. Matt 17:2), and as we look at the tabernacle or gaze on the monstrance, in a way we are gazing on Christ's humanity and divinity substantially made present, and so we are also gazing on him and his face (no. 9). The pope stated that we pray *with* Mary, our model of contemplation, this very contemplative prayer of the Rosary (nos. 10–12).

Another way to pray might be to meditate. The *Catechism* has a very good section on prayer, and it describes meditation (nos. 2705–8) aided by reading or *lectio*. The spiritual masters all speak of calming one's spirit by putting oneself in the presence of God. In the presence of the Blessed Sacrament one has only to focus on that Real Presence. In reading a passage of Scripture (e.g., one of the Gospel incidents or perhaps John 6 and its eucharistic teaching), *lectio* bids us to read slowly and allow the Word to sink in. One should mull and ponder the meaning. Meditating means allowing the Holy Spirit to take over, to take the lead. Sometimes inspiration will follow, sometimes peace, sometimes darkness. If the latter, one should simply read on. And sometimes contemplation will happen—just the awareness of the presence of God. If so, one just loves. Friends in one another's presence often don't say a lot once they've caught up—nor do lovers. Presence is enough. As the old peasant sitting in the back of the church, gazing on the tabernacle responded to the Curé of Ars (St. John Vianney) when he asked him what he was doing sitting there all day: "I look at Him and He looks at me."

Any book that nourishes prayer and meditation can be helpful. Any prayers that help one commune with God are fine. Some use the word ACTS for the ends of prayer—Adoration, Contrition, Thanksgiving, and Supplication—and proceed to do that in the presence of the Lord. First they think of all the reasons they have to *a*dore him, then all the sins for which they need to be *c*ontrite, followed by all the reasons to *t*hank God, and conclude with all their needs in *s*upplication. This personal and spontaneous meditation focuses on the various ways one relates to God. As I pray before the Lord in the Blessed Sacrament I use whatever means of prayer or meditation helps me to adore him.

TEN

THE SAINTS OF THE EUCHARIST

91. What saints encouraged eucharistic adoration?

In the nineteenth century eucharistic devotion was promoted by St. Anthony Mary Claret (1807–70). A Spanish workingman, he studied for the priesthood and was ordained in 1835. Imbued with the gift of eloquence, his popular preaching encouraged love of the Blessed Sacrament and devotion to the Immaculate Heart of the Blessed Virgin. His zeal in promoting the Gospel fostered by this devotional life was evident in his work as founder of the Claretians; as archbishop of Santiago, Cuba; in work as confessor to Queen Isabella II back in Spain; and in his printing and distribution of Catholic literature over all of Spain. His busy life ended in exile in Rome, as a participant in Vatican Council I. His love throughout his life was the Lord in the Blessed Sacrament and Our Lady.

St. Julien Eymard (1811–68) is another nineteenth-century priest who not only promoted prayer before the Blessed Sacrament but founded two orders, the Blessed Sacrament Fathers (priests) and Servants of the Blessed Sacrament (nuns) for that purpose. Ordained as a diocesan priest, he entered the Marists, but left them to found these congregations, both of which were devoted to adoration of the Blessed Sacrament but joined to other apostolates as well.

Closer to our own times is the twentieth century's Blessed Piergiorgio Frassatti (d. 1925), whom John Paul II designated as the patron of youth, having called him a "modern St. Francis," even though he was a Dominican Tertiary. A thoroughly engaging young man from a wealthy northern Italian family, he was a student, an athlete, a mountain climber, a lover of the poor, an organizer of Catholic Action, and a great lover of the Eucharist. Piergiorgio was in many ways "a golden boy" born into privilege and wealth, who mightily impressed young Karl Rahner in Germany, where Frassatti's father served as a diplomat for a time.

When he gathered young friends together for a ski trip they would
begin with Mass. He never began any day without Mass, even if
his day was packed with studies, errands to help the poor of the
city of Turin, excursions, or committee meetings, and he always
ended the day with prolonged prayer before the Blessed
Sacrament, often reciting the Rosary. He was struck down by illness at the young age of twenty-seven, this likable, well-balanced,
and attractive young saint. He has captured the popular imagina-
tion of the young and is the patron of the eucharistic movement
called Youth 2000.

All of these saints were lovers of the Eucharist and drew
from it the strength for their many activities, for their apostolate.

92. What saints nourished their contemplative life with the Eucharist?

We could single out St. Thérèse of Lisieux (1873–97) and
Blessed Elizabeth of the Trinity (1880–1906) as two nuns whose
contemplative lives were the living out of the synthesis of the
mysteries of redemption made present at Mass and prolonged in
the Liturgy of the Hours and prayer before the Blessed Sacrament.

St. Thérèse was plunged into depression at age four when her
mother died, and went through a "winter of trial" for eight years,
suffering depression, scruples, and extreme sensitivity until cured
by Our Lady. Thérèse maintained that the statue of Our Lady of
Victories smiled at her and took the place of her dead mother. At
this point, she experienced a new freedom from sensitivity, a new
love of God, a desire to even suffer for him, a desire that he be
known and loved. Her desire was to enter Carmel even though she
was too young and the local bishop would not allow it. On a pilgrimage to Rome, she broke all protocol and asked Leo XIII for
permission, and he said she would enter if it was God's will. The
way was made clear and she entered. Her two sisters had preceded
her, and they all lived under a difficult rather mercurial superior.
Thérèse avoided the politics of convent life and concentrated on

observing the rule well, of living the life of charity with her community and loving God. Her way of simplicity, of gospel living has been called her "little way," but it is the heroic way of offering all to God through Jesus. When she was sacristan, as she prepared the chalice for Mass, she sometimes wished to be a priest, but then reflecting on the various roles in the Church, the Mystical Body of Christ, she decided that the best of all as described by St. Paul was to be love in the heart of the Church—the "higher way" (cf. 1 Cor 13). The end of her short life was very painful. She suffered from tuberculosis and was plagued with temptations to deny her faith and yield to despair, but she held on valiantly to the end. Her autobiography, the *Story of a Soul,* published a year after her death, was in great demand. Her "little way" became known. She was popular with French soldiers at the front in World War I, and many felt her intercession got them home safely. She incarnated the Gospel and the cross in her time; she wrote in a nineteenth-century sentimental style, but with honesty and directness. The popularity of her approach was called "a hurricane of glory" by Pius XI, who beatified her in 1923, canonized her two years later, and praised her "little way" as a way of holiness for all types because she became a saint "without going beyond the common order of things."

Blessed Elizabeth of the Trinity was also a Carmelite nun. She also lost a parent at age four, but in this case it was her father. Her mother educated her well in the faith and exposed her to the writings of St. Teresa of Avila. At fourteen, she took a vow of virginity and at twenty-one she entered Carmel, professing her vows two years later. She was drawn to St. Teresa's phrase "in the heaven of my soul." She experienced the Holy Trinity in the cell of her heart and wanted to give herself completely in "the praise of his glory" (Eph 1:12). She saw her role, her apostolate, as enlisting all in "praise of the glory of the Holy Trinity." Her spirituality was liturgical—listening to the Word and allowing Jesus the Word to lead her to the Father: Jesus who prolongs in us his adoration of the Father and redemptive sacrifice to the Father for us. Offering herself in union with that sacrifice in "praise of his glory" was the center of her spirituality. Her model was the Blessed Virgin, particularly in the time between the annunciation and the nativity. Our Lady was attentive to the Lord within, as all Christians should be. This vocation begun for us at baptism should unfold throughout our Christian life until heaven, where all will be caught up in the unceasing praise of the Blessed of the Lamb as described in the Book of Revelation.

So we have two virgins who lived the mystery of Christ in their own time and culture, giving us an example of how to do the same in ours.

93. What saint promoted Forty Hours?

Saint Benedict Joseph Labre, the beggar saint, promoted the eucharistic devotion of Forty Hours. Born in France in 1748, the eldest of fifteen children, he studied under his uncle, the parish priest. Scripture and the lives of the saints were his favorite subjects, and he ignored his more practical studies. When his uncle died of cholera while serving the plague victims, Benedict Joseph tried to join the Trappists at eighteen, then the Carthusians, and later the Cistercians, but the young man, though good-hearted, was too eccentric to fit into a religious community. He set off to join an order in Italy, but discovered his vocation as a pilgrim for the next six years. He visited Loretto, Assisi, Einsiedeln, Aix, and Cospostella, traveling on foot with only a ragged cloak for warmth and a few books. When alms were given him, he shared them with other beggars. Homeless and with little care for his body, in 1776 he settled in Rome, passing nights in the Coliseum and days in prayer before the Blessed Sacrament in the various churches and basilicas of Rome. Whenever he heard that the Forty Hours devotion was being held in a church, he rushed there to pray before the Blessed Sacrament, earning him the title after his death as the Saint of Forty Hours. Death came in the poorhouse in

Holy Week of 1783. Acclaimed a saint by the people, the beggar saint was canonized in 1883.

94. Who was the pope of the Eucharist?

Pope St. Pius X, born in 1835, was ordained in 1858. He did pastoral work for seventeen years before becoming spiritual director of the local seminary. He took great interest in the dignity and beauty of the liturgy. While at the seminary, he directed the Gregorian choir. It comes as no surprise, then, that both as bishop of Mantua and later as patriarch of Venice, he forbade operatic and theatrical music at Mass and encouraged Gregorian chant instead. Elected pope in 1903, he issued an instruction on the liturgy, *Tra le Sollecitudini,* encouraging "active participation" in the Mass and Gregorian chant. In 1911, he established the Pontifical Institute of Sacred Music to this same end. His *Synodus Tridentina* of 1905 shocked many Catholics who were used to receiving Communion once a year (Easter Duty) or perhaps once a month (first Friday) by encouraging frequent Communion, even *daily,* if people were free of serious sin and observed the eucharistic fast. Equally shocking was his *Quam Singulari* of 1910, which allowed First Communion after first confession at the age of reason (seven) if children could know that the Communion host wasn't ordinary bread, but Jesus. The ordinary age before this had been thirteen or fourteen, around the time of confirmation, so this was a great change. Liturgically, he also reformed the Breviary, taught on the priesthood, and opposed modernism, but it is his eucharistic teaching for which he is chiefly known, so we can call him the pope of the Eucharist.

95. What saint could be called the doctor of the Eucharist?

Saint Thomas Aquinas (1225–74) could be called the doctor of the Eucharist, not only because he composed the hymns for the Office of Corpus Christi and selected the readings and such for the Mass and office of this feast, but also because of his stellar teaching on this great sacrament. Born into a noble Italian family, he was educated by the Benedictines at Monte Cassino, and it was thought that he would be abbot there. He was inclined, instead, to join the new group of preaching friars, or Dominicans, whom he met at the University of Naples. Although this move was strenuously opposed by his family, he eventually entered the Dominican order and studied for them under St. Albert the Great in Paris and Cologne. He taught theology in Paris and in Italy, where he was given a companion/secretary, Reginald of Piperno. In putting together his famous *Summa,* he saw Christ as our way back to the Father, especially through the virtuous life aided by grace and the sacraments. The Eucharist was the greatest and central sacrament, toward which the other six were directed. He masterfully defended and elucidated the doctrine of transubstantiation, as we have seen. He celebrated Mass each day, but after Mass on December 6, 1273, he stopped writing because all he wrote seemed "as straw" in comparison to what he had experienced during Mass that day. He died on his way to the reunion Council of Lyons, and on his deathbed, he said before the Blessed Sacrament held aloft as Viaticum: "I receive you, price of my soul's salvation; all my studies and my labors have been for love of you. I submit all that I have written to your holy Church in whose obedience I now pass from this earth."

ELEVEN

THE ESCHATOLOGICAL DIMENSION
OF THE EUCHARIST

96. What is the heavenly liturgy?

In the Book of Revelation, a glorious scene is depicted with the Lord as a Lamb, slain and yet still standing, that is, risen on his throne. Twenty-four elders are bowing in adoration, laying their crowns before him. Billows of incense rise and great torches are burning, while heavenly music resounds: "Worthy is the Lamb...to receive...honor and glory..." (Rev 5:12). For us this invokes the great chorus of Handel's *Messiah,* but the great composer was himself trying to do justice to this heavenly liturgy.

Some scripture scholars would say that the human author, St. John, described the heavenly scene in the light of the Jewish-Christian liturgy he knew at the time: twenty-four elders on the semicircular bench, or bema, venerating the paschal Lamb on the chair of Moses, or the chair of authority in the synagogue, with the Temple imagery of incense, candles, and music thrown in as well. It could be so, but since "no eye has seen, nor ear heard...what God has prepared for those who love him" (1 Cor 2:9), heaven can only be described symbolically anyway. We must wait and see. Because music and singing figure so prominently in these descriptions, some have suggested that purgatory will be a choir practice!

Because the Eucharist is a sign of Christ's Body and Blood, it will not exist in heaven, but Christ alone will, the reality toward which the sign points. For in heaven we will see him "face to face" (1 Cor 13:12), and this participation in the beatific vision (CCC no. 1023) brings us beyond the need of any signs or symbols because we have gone beyond them and are face to face with the reality of the triune God, the goal of our pilgrimage. The sacramental veils are lifted and we share in his glory, "...when every tear will be wiped away. On that day we shall see you, our God, as you are. We shall become like you and praise you forever through Christ our Lord" (Eucharistic Prayer III: Commemoration of the Dead).

97. What are the eschatological dimensions of the Eucharist?

First we must ask what the word "eschatological" means. It comes from the Greek word *eschaton,* meaning "the end-time" or "the end of time." It refers to the end of time on earth, but also since that includes the "new heavens and a new earth" (2 Pet 3:13), it means the heavenly dimension as well. We have looked at the heavenly liturgy and can see the earthly liturgy as a mirror image of that in heaven. This aspect is especially emphasized by the Eastern churches. In the Byzantine Rite, the Iconostasis, which we in the West see as a barrier (a wall of icons separating the sanctuary and altar from the nave), the East sees as a golden bridge joining heaven and earth. The background of all the saints in the icons is golden, because that is the color of eternity where the saints now dwell. We've discussed how the Jewish notion of memorial brings the past event into the present for the sake of the future. At Mass, or the Divine Liturgy, the past events of Christ's death and resurrection are brought into the present as he is really and sacramentally made present on the altar, the same "Lamb on the throne" who is in heaven. So in a way, heaven comes to earth each time the Eucharist is celebrated, and yet it has not come in its fullness, for the end of time has not yet come.

While on earth in this life we *already* participate in the life given us in the Eucharist, yet the fullness of that life has *not yet* come. And so we pray: "O Sacred Banquet, in which Christ becomes our food, the memory of his Passion is renewed, the soul is filled with grace, and a pledge of future glory is given" (Magnificat Antiphon for Corpus Christi: Evening Prayer II in the Liturgy of the Hours).

98. Does the Eucharist help those in purgatory? What is purgatory?

The *Catechism* echoes the tradition of the Church (defined at Trent) that Mass or the "Eucharistic sacrifice is also offered for *the faithful departed* who 'have died in Christ but are not yet wholly purified...'" (no. 1371), and goes on to give the witness of Saint Monica (d. 387) as a confirmation of this practice: "Put this body anywhere! Don't trouble yourselves about it! I simply ask you to remember me at the Lord's altar wherever you are" (*Confessions* 9:13 quoted in CCC no. 1371).

The traditional reading for the anniversary Mass for the Dead is from the Second Book of Maccabees (which our Protestant brethren do not accept as inspired) in which Judas, the leader of the Maccabean revolt against the pagan rule of his time, offered sacrifice for those fallen in battle and "made atonement for the dead, so that they might be delivered from their sin" (12:45). The Church now offers the sacrifice of the Mass for those in purgatory as it is a "holy and pious thought" to pray for the dead (ibid.).

Purgatory is the name the Church gives to that state of purgation for those who die in a state of friendship with God (i.e., in a state of grace) but who are in need of purification, for "nothing unclean will enter it [God's presence]" (Rev 21:27). The Church has not defined it as a place but does allude to a purifying fire (cf. 1 Cor 3:13; CCC no. 1031), though not specifying what kind of fire (spiritual, symbolic, physical, etc.) this might be. St. Catherine of Genoa (d. 1510) sees the souls in purgatory as rushing toward this purgation, so eager are they to be cleansed and come into God's presence. Those in purgatory are saved; they are numbered among the elect, but have not yet begun to enjoy the beatific vision. Our prayers and sacrifices hasten them to that end, so that they in turn may pray for us. The Eastern Orthodox churches do not believe in purgatory, though they do hold for a top layer of hell from which there is escape to heaven after purification by fire—which amounts to the same thing. Let us give the last word to a father from the East, St. John

Chrysostom: "Let us help and commemorate them. If Job's sons were purified by their father's sacrifice why should we doubt that our offerings for the dead bring them some consolation? Let us not hesitate to help those who have died and to offer our prayers for them" (quoted in CCC no. 1032).

99. Is the liturgy cosmic?

John Paul II responded, "Yes cosmic! Because even when it is celebrated on the humble altar of a country church, the Eucharist is always in some way celebrated *on the altar of the world*. It unites heaven and earth" (E.E., no. 8).

In the Book of Revelation's heavenly liturgy, which we have discussed, all creation according to the *Catechism* is "recapitulated in Christ": All are taken up in the great high priestly prayer of the God-Man, Jesus Christ; the heavenly powers; the four living creatures (representing all creation); the twenty-four elders (representing the Old and New Covenants); the one hundred forty-four thousand (representing the People of God, especially the martyrs); Our Lady (the woman clothed with the sun, crowned with stars and with the moon under her feet); and the great multitude, which no one could number, from every nation, from all tribes, peoples, and tongues (cf. Rev 4–7, 12, 21).

All creatures and even all creation celebrate this cosmic, this heavenly and eternal liturgy whenever they participate in the sacramental and earthly liturgy below, for in Christ's paschal mystery heaven and earth are joined. Material being is being made ready—transformed into the "new heavens and a new earth" (2 Pet 3:13), when in the fullness of time the Lord will hand over the kingdom of his priestly people to the Father and God will be all in all (1 Cor 15:28). And so the *Exultet* exclaims:

> Rejoice, heavenly powers! Sing, choirs of angels!
> Exult, all creation around God's throne!
> Jesus Christ, our King, is risen!
> Sound the trumpet of salvation!

100. Do the angels and saints participate in this liturgy?

The icon painter Adé Bethune (d. 2002) used to say that rather than throwing out all statues of the saints from our churches, they ought to ring the altar on the other side from the congregation to show that as Christ, the great high priest, comes to our altar in the Eucharist, the heavenly liturgy with the saints and angels does as well. All of our prefaces speak of the angels, who join us in singing the "Holy, holy, holy" or *Sanctus*. The Tridentine prefaces listed them as well—with angels and archangels, thrones and dominations, virtues, powers, and principalities, cherubim and seraphim—all nine choirs of angels join the assembly on earth in singing the praise of God, through Christ and in the Spirit. We on earth, as we celebrate, are in union with all the saints in heaven, as John Paul II reminded us: "[With] Mary, the ever Virgin Mother of Jesus Christ, our Lord and God, the angels, the holy apostles, the glorious martyrs and all the saints. This is an aspect of the Eucharist which merits greater attention: in celebrating the sacrifice of the Lamb, we are united to the heavenly liturgy....[T]he Eucharist is truly a glimpse of heaven appearing on earth" (E.E. no. 19).

And so Our Lady sings the Magnificat, as an ancient hymn goes, and the "Te Deum" lists the apostles praising the triune God along with the prophets, the martyrs, as well as the whole Church throughout the world. Here the heavenly choirs of the great cloud of witnesses who have gone before us (Heb. 12:1) join the earthly assembly in their song of praise.

101. How is the Eucharist a foretaste of heaven?

At the Last Supper, the Lord himself tied the Eucharist he was instituting with its fulfillment in the kingdom: "I tell you, I will never again drink of this fruit of the vine until that day when I drink it new with you in my Father's kingdom" (Matt 26:29). Whenever the Church celebrates the Eucharist, which makes Christ present and joins us to him, the Church "turns her gaze to 'him who is to come' and calls out 'Come Lord Jesus' praying that the fulfillment of the Eucharistic promise of a more complete and lasting union with the Lord will come and that quickly" (cf. CCC no. 1403; Rev 1:4; 22:20; 1 Cor 16:22).

Let us sum up with the *Catechism:*

> There is no surer pledge or clearer sign of this great hope in the new heavens and the new earth (2 Peter 3:13)…than the Eucharist. Every time this mystery is celebrated "the work of our redemption is carried on" (L.G. no. 3) and we "break the one bread that provides the medicine of immortality, the antidote for death, and the food that makes us live forever in Jesus Christ" (St. Ignatius's Letter to the Ephesians 20, 2; quoted in the CCC, no. 1405).

FOR FURTHER READING

Bouyer, Louis. *The Eucharist*. Notre Dame, Indiana: Notre Dame Press, 1968.

Corbon, Jean. *The Wellspring of Worship*. New York/Mahwah, New Jersey: Paulist Press, 1988.

Deiss, Lucien. *The Springtime of the Liturgy*. Collegeville, Minnesota: Liturgical Press, 1979.

Elliott, Peter. *Ceremonies of the Modern Roman Rite*. San Francisco: Ignatius Press, 1993.

Emminghaus, J. *The Eucharist*. Collegeville, Minnesota: Liturgical Press, 1978.

Guardini, R. *Sacred Signs*. Wilmington, Delaware: Michael Glazier, 1979.

Irwin, Kevin. *Models of the Eucharist*. New York/Mahwah, New Jersey: Paulist Press, 2005.

Jungmann, Joseph. *The Mass*. Collegeville, Minnesota: Liturgical Press, 1975.

Klauser, T. *Short History of the Western Liturgy*. London: Oxford, 1979.

Nichols, Aidan, OP. *Looking at the Liturgy*. San Francisco: Ignatius Press, 1996.

Ratzinger, Joseph. *Feast of Faith*. San Francisco: Ignatius Press, 1986.

————. The *Spirit of the Liturgy*. San Francisco: Ignatius Press, 2000.

RESPONSES TO 101 QUESTIONS ABOUT JESUS
by Michael L. Cook, SJ

RESPONSES TO 101 QUESTIONS ON THE PSALMS
AND OTHER WRITINGS
by Roland E. Murphy, O Carm

RESPONSES TO 101 QUESTIONS ON DEATH AND
ETERNAL LIFE
by Peter C. Phan

RESPONSES TO 101 QUESTIONS ON HINDUISM
by John Renard

RESPONSES TO 101 QUESTIONS ON BUDDHISM
by John Renard

RESPONSES TO 101 QUESTIONS ON THE MASS
by Kevin W. Irwin

RESPONSES TO 101 QUESTIONS ON GOD AND EVOLUTION
by John F. Haught

RESPONSES TO 101 QUESTIONS ON
CATHOLIC SOCIAL TEACHING
by Kenneth R. Himes, OFM